Filmmakers and Financing,
Second Edition

Filmmakers and Financing
Second Edition

Business Plans
for Independents

Louise Levison

Focal Press
Boston, Oxford, Johannesburg, Melbourne, New Delhi, Singapore

Focal Press is an imprint of Butterworth–Heinemann.

Copyright © 1998 by Louise Levison

ᴿ A member of the Reed Elsevier group

 Butterworth–Heinemann supports the efforts of American For-ests and the Global ReLeaf program in its campaign for the bet-terment of trees, forests, and our environment.

Library of Congress Cataloging-in-Publication Data

Levison, Louise
    Filmmakers and financing / Louise Levison. — 2nd ed.
        p.   cm.
    Includes index.
    ISBN 0-240-80300-0 (alk. paper)
    1. Motion pictures—Production and direction.   2. Motion picture
industry—Finance.   I. Title.
PN1995.9.P7L433   1998
791.43'0232'0681—dc21   97-13434
                                                                 CIP

British Library Cataloguing-in-Publication Data
A catalogue record for this book is available from the British Library.

The publisher offers special discounts on bulk orders of this book.
For information, please contact:

    Manager of Special Sales
    Butterworth–Heinemann
    225 Wildwood Avenue
    Woburn, MA 01801–2041
    Tel: (781) 904-2500
    Fax: (781) 904-2620

For information on all Focal Press publications available, contact our World Wide Web home page at: http://www.bh.com/focalpress

10 9 8 7 6 5 4 3 2

Printed in the United States of America

To my special mother, whose support cheers me on,
and my beloved father, the ultimate entrepreneur.

Contents

Foreword

Despite the near hero-worship accorded successful independent film producers and studio executives, not one of them would be able to function without a strong backup team. The myth of the one-person band is just that—a myth. Without the talent and hard work of the lawyers, bankers, accountants, development personnel, and administrative staff—not to mention the literally hundreds of people involved in actually making the films—no independent producer could survive, much less succeed.

To marshal all the disparate talents involved in mounting a major film production, the most important element is a common vision of the ultimate end product. In the same way that directors need a storyboard to communicate their vision of what the film will look like, producers need their own version of a storyboard (that is, a business plan) to explain their objectives, hopes, aspirations, and, yes, even their dreams.

Gone are the days when a business plan was regarded as inappropriate for an artistic endeavor, such as producing a film. These days, the risks are too large, the competition too intense, and the sophistication of investors too great to "leave the details until later." Completion guarantees, discounted cash flows, letters of credit, foreign sales contracts, domestic distribution deals, internal rates of return, gross deals, rolling breaks, third-party participants' security interest, bank discounting, residuals, cross-collateralization—all these terms, to name just a few, have become part of the regular vocabulary of today's independent producers. Without a detailed business plan to coordinate all these elements, it would be virtually impossible to produce a major film. So, dear independent producer, read on. . . .

Jake Eberts

Acknowledgments

To all the clients and students who have taught me as much as I have taught them

To all the industry professionals who have generously given of their time in classes and seminars to share their knowledge

To Jake Eberts for graciously contributing to this book

To Michael Donaldson, Greg Bernstein, Bill Whitacre, Harlan Schneider, Dr. Linda Seger, John Johnson, Robert W. Fisher, Rick Pamplin, and Howard K. Grossman whose comments on and contributions to the text are greatly appreciated

To the staff of the Entertainment Studies Department of UCLA, especially Ronnie Rubin and Debra Magit, for helping an entrepreneur make her way through the academic maze

To Suzy Prudden for helping me keep my mind/body in balance while spending hours at the computer

To Ginger at Jerry's and everyone at The Coffee Roaster for helping feed the body as well as the mind

To Bill, Helen, Jeffrey, and Carl for their support and understanding

To Faryl Reingold for her editorial contributions and comments

To my editors at Focal Press, Marie Lee, Tammy F. Harvey, and Karen E. Sadowski, for their patience and understanding

And last, but not least, to Leonard the Wonder Cat for his personal inspiration for the cat tales and for his willingness to supervise the entire writing process from the perspective of my lap.

_____ Introduction
Controlling Your Destiny

If a man does not know which way he is headed, no wind is the right wind.

SENECA

WHY SHOULD YOU BUY THIS BOOK?

King Ferdinand of Spain appointed a group of consultants to advise him on Christopher Columbus's enterprise for sailing to the Indies. This scholarly group of astronomers, mariners, and pilots pored over charts and graphs. They determined not only that the world was flat, but also that the ocean was too big to be conquered.

"Ergo," they said, "if you try to sail to the Indies, you will fail." But Columbus had done his homework and planned ahead. He replied, "I have researched my own charts and graphs, spoken to other sailors, and obtained years of technical experience that proves otherwise. I believe it can be done." Columbus was the prototypical entrepreneur. He examined his proposed business venture, made forecasts regarding pros and cons and plunder versus expenses, and then he decided to move ahead.

From the dawn of film—actually, from the dawn of time—there have been individuals who have wanted to do it their own way. People who are not content to live by another's rules continually strike out on their own. As we approach the year 2000, corporations are shrinking the size of their staffs, and the number of independent players is growing.

Neither Columbus nor any of his friends or enemies knew that he would run into the Americas on his journey. Nevertheless, he seized his opportunity and took appropriate action. By keeping abreast of the situation on the ships and the changes in the outside environment, he was able to make an informed decision. When he landed in the wrong place, Columbus looked at the opportunity, measured it against his goals, and decided to make the most of it.

Tactics for a Constantly Changing Medium

My friend Jerry Quigg suggested calling this book *sex, films, and investing*. Good title. It is clear, informative, and to the point. All the elements for a book or a business plan are there. Your finest hour will come when an investor says, "What a sexy idea! It will make me money. How much do you want?" This book is sexy, too, in its own businesslike way. It will bridge the gap for you between the passion of filmmaking and the day-to-day realities of creating a successful company.

As you read this, the motion picture business is changing right before your eyes. Studios have a shifting focus. Three years ago the Japanese manufacturers of hardware components were buying major studios and cable and telephone companies were bidding for those left to control as much of the information superhighway as possible. Now the studios are looking for half or more of their productions funds to come from outside investors, Seagrams bought MCA from Matsushita, and the cable/telephone conglomerates are fighting among themselves.

Analysts predict that the "paradigm" (current in-vogue word meaning "pattern") of the motion picture business will change, but opinions differ as to how. Some things about the film world are not likely to change. Movies will continue to be major entertainment, and people will continue to make them. All those hungry monoliths will look to independents for their product. No matter how many times the corporations divide the finite viewing audience among different technological choices, theatrical motion pictures will still chug down the track. Product will be needed to fuel that engine, and your company may be the one to provide it.

People go into independent filmmaking for many reasons. They are driven primarily by the subject matter, theme, or style of the pictures they want to make. I have talked to hundreds of people who have told me what types of films they want to make, and no two people have had the same vision or goals. They all share one particular goal, though—to own their project and control it. Once a filmmaker forms a company for that purpose, it is up to him or her to understand how the business world functions. Of course, your goal may not be feature films at all. Instead, you may focus on other types of films, videos, or other products. All of these are important, and all the principles stated in this book apply equally to them.

With new opportunities appearing for the independent film-maker, more and more people want their own companies. Books and articles have been written about the ins and outs of writing or finding the perfect script, how much it costs to make a film, finding the best location, and what camera to use. None of that information is in this book. The question before us is not how to make a film, but how to get the money to make one—or rather, many of them. We are dealing with how to create and finance a company.

You might argue, "But I'm making *films*. This is different from other businesses." The details of business may differ from industry to industry and from segment to segment, but the principles are the same. Movies involve lots of people, all of whom expect to get paid. Raising money involves intermediaries such as agents, finders, and lawyers, who expect to get a fee for what they do—and do not forget the investor, who hopes to see a return on the investment. All companies need certain standard ingredients to get going and stay alive. To get the show on the road, you need to put together a business plan.

It is true that many firms have been launched and gone on to success without a business plan. Many more firms without one, however, have failed. Just read the newspaper or turn on the television. Owners start undercapitalized and go downhill from there. No plan can guarantee the thrill of victory, but not having a plan will bring you closer to the agony of defeat.

When you read about all those production companies setting up shop with a large influx of capital from some foreign source, which of these scenarios do you believe?

1. SCENARIO 1: Louise, you've had such extraordinary success at Megalomaniac Studios that we would like to give you $100 million. Have fun and send us our share.
2. SCENARIO 2: Louise, you've had such extraordinary success at Megalomaniac Studios that we would like to explore the possibility of having you head your own company with $100-million seed capital. Why don't you get together with Victor Visionary from Major Merge Investment Group and create a business plan. If we agree with your product analysis and the numbers look good, we're in business.

Trust me (famous Hollywood term), scenario 2 is far more likely. People do not throw around big bucks on a whim. The original idea— "Louise looks good; let's have her run a production company for us"—may be a whim. Before that impulse becomes a reality, however, much thinking and analysis will be done. All that reflection put on paper in the proper form is—you guessed it—a business plan.

The purpose of this book is to show you how to make all that thinking and analyzing into a coherent story. It is more than just an outline, however. The standard business plan outline has not changed in the past 30 years. Open any book on business planning and you will see

- Summary
- Company
- Product
- Marketing
- Selling
- Financing

The question is not the formula, but what do you do next? This book will help you take the next step to expound and polish your business plan within those guidelines. It specifies not only what you need to include, but also why and how. I will give you samples—both good and bad—for writing the individual sections of your business plan. In the rest of this introduction, we will explore the reason for going through these exercises.

Movies as a Business

The biggest misconception about the movie business is that the *movie* is more important than the *business*. Many of us tend to think about filmmaking, not as a business at all, but as an art form; in that case, it would be called *show art* instead of *show business*.

A movie *is* a form of art, but a very expensive one. The most difficult concept for filmmakers often is looking at the movie as a commercial enterprise. The word *commercial* can be viewed in two very different ways. When it comes to artistic endeavors, many people give the word a negative connotation. The strict definition is "prepared for sale," but in many people's minds, the words "without regard to quality" are added to the end of that definition. Looking at it in the broader sense, however, the filmmaker trades a seat at the film for someone else's dollar (or $4 or $7 as the case may be). Whether this trade occurs at a multiplex mall theater or at a video store, the buyer expects to get value for the trade, and value is definitely in the eye of the beholder.

When *Sling Blade* received an Academy Award nomination for Best Adapted Screenplay and another for Billy Bob Thornton for Best Actor, one of the critics said that it was just another commercial, predictable film. Makes you wonder what films he's been watching, doesn't it? Even Billy Bob Thornton, the writer–director–actor, thought it would garner a small audience. It combined several factors that blocked funds from production companies—a mentally defective, ax-murderer lead character and a nontraditional ending. The film's eventual box office success does not take away from its origins as a $1.35 million production financed by The Shooting Gallery, which up to that time had been providing finishing funds and an incubator-type workplace. If the movie had earned only $5 million at the box office, it could still be considered commercial compared to the budget level. And Miramax's $10 million acquisition payment did not change the film's independent status.

There are plenty of successful filmmakers who manage to find their own financing to do things their way—Thornton, John Sayles, the Coen brothers, Jim Jarmusch, and Henry Jaglom, to name a few. They make films on whatever subjects please them. Their films may have a limited distribution, but the directors (who often are also the writers) have their own financing. They keep their budgets at levels comparable to the likely box office receipts.

John Sayles has had many critical successes, such as *Return of the Secaucus Seven, Brother from Another Planet, City of Hope,* and *Passion Fish*. These films were financed by Sayles' own investors. Although critical hits, his first big commercial hit is 1996's *Lone Star*. Similarly, the Coen brothers' independently made *Fargo* was their first major box office winner, despite earlier critical successes such as *Raising Arizona*.

It seems to be a simple concept. If you produce a gizmo designed to lose money, you go out of business. Why would it be any different with a film? Many films lose money (ask the studios), but most filmmakers intend to have some success. Film investors have a right to expect to make back their money, at least. Unfortunately, many auteur filmmakers find creativity and attracting an audience mutually exclusive. If you suffer from this malady, try to reeducate yourself. Even relatives have their limits.

Investors now have a right to expect nonfiction films, such as documentaries and concert films, to make a profit. These films have gained a strong presence at the theatrical box office in recent years. The success of *Roger and Me* in 1989 began the reemergence of the nonfiction film as a credible theatrical release. After a few successful films in the intervening years, 1994's *Hoop Dreams* attracted a lot of attention by reaching U.S. box office receipts of $7.8 million with a budget of $800,000. The same year *Crumb* reached a total of $3 million on a budget of $300,000. And in March 1997, *When We Were Kings*, a documentary on the Muhammad Ali–George Foreman fight in Zaire 23 years ago, which won an Academy Award, is on its way to becoming the first financially successful Oscar winner for Best Documentary in recent history.

People Get the Money

A frequent question asked me by students and clients is, "How much money have your business plans raised?" My answer is, "None. People raise money. Business plans are only a tool." Three of the best business plans I ever wrote are filed in drawers; they haven't raised any money. In addition, although you may have the best written and presented business plan ever done, to raise the money you have to (1) be ready to go ahead with the business, (2) understand the premise, and (3) be professional.

To be ready to get your project off the ground, you have to be focused on your goal. If you are arguing with your partners, are not ready to make decisions, or are unwilling to look for money, the quality of your business plan is immaterial. From the biggest consulting firms down to the smallest ones, there are plans stored on shelves gathering dust, because the client company was not ready to be serious about taking on partners or making changes. Business plans do not find money by themselves.

Once you track down your prey and deliver this terrific plan, you have to explain what it is all about—how it represents you. A plan is only a guideline with strategies and forecasts. You have to demonstrate to others that you can carry out the steps described within. Unless you understand every step of the plan—rather than just handing over a document written by someone else—you will not be able to do this.

Finally, are you adept at handling business in a professional and impressive manner? When all is said and done, the company is only a reflection of your demeanor and presentation. After all the numbers have been added up, investors are still betting on people. If they are unsure or wary about you, no checks will be written.

All consultants have clients that they would like to keep hidden away. Sometimes it would be ideal if the entrepreneur and the investor never met. Some clients like to argue with investors and generally have a take-it-or-leave-it attitude. I once had a client who actually said to an investor, "I'm doing you a favor by giving you this opportunity. Take it or leave it." The investor left it.

Can Anybody Do This?

Developing a business plan involves the proverbial "10 percent inspiration and 90 percent perspiration." Anybody can do it. Unfortunately, I have found that most people lose interest when faced with the amount of research and work that is required. If you want to start your own company, however, this is part of the price of admission.

To find financing for your films, you do not have to be part of the business world; you do not have to be an M.B.A. or an accounting genius. The business plan bridges the gap between right-brain creative thinking and the left-brain math stuff. All it requires is the desire and a passion for the product. Being in control of your own destiny is a powerful enough motivation.

Hollywood Is Only an Attitude

This book does not restrict the term *filmmaker* to those toiling in the hills of Hollywood. Movie-making is a nationwide and worldwide event. The person in Cincinnati with a camcorder who aspires to make a documentary or a feature film is as much a filmmaker as his or her counterpart in Hollywood. John Sayles lives and works in New Jersey. Watch the film festival rosters and you will quickly see that there is more movie-making going on outside of Hollywood than in it. Consider the following examples.

My clients Bob Fisher and Rick Pamplin lived and worked in Hollywood for a number of years. Rick sold projects to both studios and independent production companies, taught screenwriting, and produced and directed an independent film. Bob worked for Samuel Z. Arkoff and has screen credits on Universal's *Darkroom* and several other scripts. To do their own thing, however, they left Hollywood proper and moved to Orlando, Florida. We worked together to put their goals and objectives into a financial package. It took lots of leg work for them to find interested investors; now they have their own consortium of money people from the local area and several heartland states. They recently made *Michael Winslow Live*, which was entered by the Directors Guild of America in the Florida Film Festival, and are in pre-production on *Hoover*.

Jon Jost, from San Francisco, writes and directs films under his own company banner. He has made more than 11 independently financed films, such as *Sure Fire* and *All the Vermeers in New York*. Shot in different locations around the country, his films have won awards in both the United States and abroad, including the Berlin Film Festival Award and the L.A. Critics' Award for best independent/experimental film.

The moral of these stories is that "Hollywood" is not a specific place. Film commissions make sure of that. Living outside the environs of Los Angeles and New York is no longer a hindrance to success in this business. You need not be in those cities to meet the important players in the film industry. You might find them at a film festival or a market or simply at the other end of the phone. Fiberoptic technology is now arriving on the scene. Fiber-optic cable is a glass or plastic cable that allows you to send images over the telephone lines. Its carrying capacity is much greater than that of coaxial cable. It allows a producer to be in one location and the background scenes, the actors, or both in other locations. No one has to travel anywhere. For example, for the movie *Searching for Bobby Fischer*, Ben Kingsley's looping (the actor repeating his lines when dialogue is not clear) was done while he was in London and the producer and editors were in Los Angeles. Until now the actor has had to be in the studio watching the screen in order to synchronize the words. It took eight telephone exchanges each way, but that type of problem will be ironed out as more phone companies pursue fiber-optic technology.

An Entrepreneur Is an Entrepreneur Is . . .

For most entrepreneurs, the idea of boiling down a vision into a neatly contained business proposal is as foreign as the notion of taking a job. Nevertheless, the recipe for success in today's competitive business environment demands that we become managers as well as artists. The most common blunder that entrepreneurs make is to assume that a business plan is a creative piece of fiction you use to trick a bank officer into giving you money. Even worse is the assumption that creating a business plan is an interesting hobby for someone who has nothing else to do. The biggest mistake made by independent film-makers is to see themselves not as business people, but as artistes—creatures whose contact with the murky world of business is tangential to their filmmaking and unimportant. Nothing could be further from the truth.

When a person has an original idea and develops it into a product, an entrepreneur is born—a person who has personal drive, creates an intimate vision, and is willing to take risks. Entrepreneurs want to make the decisions and be in charge of the show; they want to do what they want to do when they want to do it! I have never met an entrepreneur who was not convinced that she was right, who did not believe that the world couldn't live without her film, and who did not want to control her own destiny. Independent filmmakers are the best kinds of entrepreneurs, because they want to push the edge of the envelope and seek new horizons. They are the major risk-takers.

Film investors are the biggest risk-takers of all, however. They bet their dollars on an idea and help it become a reality—a contribution not to be taken lightly. Too often filmmakers believe that investors should donate their money and then quietly go away. Of course, this attitude is not unique to filmmakers. Most entrepreneurs feel that their ideas have more value than the capital needed to make them a reality. Think again, or you won't see any cash.

WHY BOTHER WITH A BUSINESS PLAN?

The business plan is the entrepreneur's single most valuable document and his best safeguard for success. The majority of businesses that fail usually have paid little attention to proper planning. In Jake Eberts' book, *My Indecision Is Final: The Rise and Fall of Goldcrest Films*, he mentions several times that the company had no business plan. Although their first film, *Chariots of Fire*, won the Academy Award for Best Picture, the company (different from the one in operation today) did not succeed in the long run. Would Goldcrest have fared differently had there been one? No one can say for sure, but it is obvious in reading the book that a group of very talented people got together with different professional and personal agendas. They also had very different business styles.

A business plan is a must for a new company (or an expanding one). It gives you the opportunity to develop a clear picture of the growth and bottom-line prospects for your film company. It enables you to make more effective decisions, and it helps everyone follow the leader. When you have a path laid out, you have guideposts to follow that will show where you are vis-à-vis your goals. The secondary purpose of the business plan is to show the investor that you know what you are doing.

The ideal length and depth of a business plan varies from business to business. This is true if you are building a shoe factory or making *Nightmare on Elm Street 26*. You have something to accomplish and a specific path you must travel to accomplish it. The steps that you take along that path are defined in your plan.

Before beginning any business, you want to know the nature of your goals and objectives, the desired size of the company, the products and/or services it will sell, its customers and market niche, the amount of revenue likely to flow, and its sources. Whether you hope to start a full-fledged production company or just make one film, you have to identify who you are, where you are going, and how you are going to get there.

When you think of business plans, your first thought may be how to impress the investor. Before you worry about the bank or the distribution company or the wealthy investor, however, you have to make a personal business plan. For all of those people—and for yourself—you have to come up with an agreeable course of action, and you have to stick to it. This book will help you do that.

Do You Really Need a Business Plan?

Before you actually begin to create a business plan, consider your actions for a minute. Is a business plan what you want? Answer these questions:

1. Are you packaging one film for a studio sale?
2. Are you raising money for one film or a group of films?
3. Do you want to be responsible for the organization, management, and payroll of a business?
4. Are you willing to keep track of everything going on in the company, or do you plan to turn all responsibility over to someone else?

Be honest with yourself. What is it that you really want to do? A full business plan is necessary for a real company—not just to show potential investors what a "can't-miss" investment it is, but also to put on paper for yourself the direction of your work. It means being more than just a producer or director; it means planning ahead three to five years for a company that will make a succession of films; it means optioning or writing enough properties to make the company valid; it means having around you a talented team to which you will delegate responsibility. Most of all, it means accepting responsibility for everything that goes on in the company, from the logo to the bank account.

Does a Single Film Need a Business Plan?

Single films also require a business plan. These are exactly the same as large company plans, except you have fewer numbers to project. The results of one film will take you out three years from beginning of development to 80% of your revenues being returned. It is essential to remember that before going into business, you must find out for yourself if business is your thing. One film is a business, and the producer (or executive producer) is the manager. You have the same responsibility to investors as if you were making four or five films. Going through this book will help you determine if a business is what you really want

The Facts and Nothing But . . .

The structure for a business plan is standard, but the contents are not boilerplate. Each film company or project has its own unique qualities. All plans must be substantive, promotional, and succinct, with a length generally between 25 and 50 pages—that is, comprehensive but not too long. The most important aspect of business plans is that they contain enough information in a readable format that they excite, or at least impress, potential investors. Most of all, the plan should represent you and your ideas. Copying someone else's plan is like copying someone's test paper in school. You may give the right answers to the wrong questions.

A few years ago, a friend of mine wrote a business plan that was very professional and cleverly laid out. He found that he had to keep it under lock and key because other producers kept making copies of it. What they failed to recognize was the specialized nature of his company. It was structured to develop films—à la Interscope—not produce them. The people who copied the business plan all had production companies. They were so enamored of the text and graphics that they were blinded to the obvious: The business plan promoted a type of company that they did not plan to run. How did they ever manage to answer investors' questions?

ABOUT THIS BOOK

Whether you use this book as a step-by-step guide for writing a plan or as a test of your own ability to be in business, it will help meld creative thought with business fundamentals. It has been written in language that is accessible to those who are not skillful with business jargon. Understanding business is not that hard. Whether you want to take the time to learn about business or even want to be bothered with the noncreative aspects of filmmaking is another question. You will have to answer that for yourself.

What if, after reading this book, you decide you would be better off selling your script to a studio or directing for one? Have you wasted your money? No. You will have saved money by reading this book first. It is better to find out now, rather than several months or thousands of dollars down the road, that the business life is not for you.

Business Plan Outline

This book is best described as a movie within a movie. To find financing for your projects, you will have to describe how your company will function. Accordingly, this book describes the system of marketing and financing individual films within the greater framework of the film company.

The book is arranged so that the numbered chapters follow the steps of the business plan. They appear in the order that the sections of your plan should follow:

1. Executive Summary
2. The Company
3. The Products
4. The Industry
5. The Market
6. Distribution
7. Financing
8. The Financial Plan

Finally, a sample business plan for a fictional company appears in the appendix. Note that the subheadings in these chapters do not have to appear in the business plan.

This outline has been the stuff of business plans from time immemorial. No matter how independent you are, when writing your business plan, do not fool with tradition. You should make it as easy as you can for potential investors to read your plan. They are used to seeing the information in a certain way, so humor them. It is in your best interest not to be an auteur with your business plan.

As you devise your plan section by section, you will find yourself being repetitious; likewise, you will find the chapters of this book somewhat repetitious.

Think of the plan as a series of building blocks. Starting with the second section, you will describe the members of your company and explain what you are all about. Next, you will talk about your products in exhaustive detail. Then, to set the background, you will describe the industry as a whole. Once you have set the milieu within which you function, you will show the market potential of your products. In the section on distribution, you will explain the methods and potential of issuing your products in the different markets. Finally, you will explain the financial methods and how the company is going to make money.

To put it another way, in the first few sections, you will explain *what* the company is; the rest of the plan will consist of all the *hows*. I skipped over the executive summary. As that is covered in the next chapter, I will not spoil the surprise. Suffice it to say that the first section of the plan is exactly what it says it is—a summary of everything else in the plan.

Goals of This Book

My goal in writing this book is to give you, the independent filmmaker, an introduction to the world of business and to provide a format to help you present yourself and your projects in the best possible light. There are many filmmakers with projects who are struggling to obtain equity (partnership) dollars. Being able to see your project from the investor's viewpoint and being able to present it to the financial community in a recognizable form will give you a useful edge on the competition.

Throughout the book, I emphasize that this is your plan. People want to know who *you* are and what you will do. Dreams are good;

the nature of an entrepreneur is to be a dreamer. Your plan will bring the dream and the reality together.

Disclaimer

To make the book clearer, many examples of business plans are presented. In some cases, I have quoted from existing business plans and indicate as much. In most cases, though, I have invented names of people, movies, and companies as a literary device. Given the number of production companies and movies that appear and disappear every day, I may accidentally have selected a name you use or propose to use. Such an occurrence is purely coincidental.

1

Executive Summary

"Begin at the beginning," the King said, gravely, "and go till you come to the end; then stop."

LEWIS CARROLL
Alice's Adventures in Wonderland

READ THIS CHAPTER LAST!

This admonition is like saying, "Don't open this package until Christmas!" You are, right this minute, ignoring me and reading this chapter anyway. Fine, but when it comes to writing your business plan, write the Executive Summary last. The Executive Summary is the first feature your investors read and the last section you should write. It is the hook that pulls readers into your net, and it must represent your future plans precisely.

The Executive Summary is the place where you tell readers what you're about to tell them. Am I confusing you? Remember that old advice about writing term papers: "Tell them what you're going to tell them; tell them; tell them what you told them"? You do the same thing with the Executive Summary. It is a condensed version of the rest of your proposal. This is not a term paper; this is your life.

The beginning of your work is the section about your company. You give a brief overview of the people, the products, and your goals. In the rest of the sections—Product, Industry, Markets, Distribution, and Finance—you give them more detail about how the company is going to function. The last section you write is the Executive Summary, which is just that—a summary. It presents a review of the plan for the reader.

WHY WRITE THE SUMMARY LAST?

Developing a business plan is a process of discovery. Until you actually put your business plan together, you cannot be sure what it will contain. As you will see in reading the rest of this book, much research, thought, and skill goes into a proposal of this type. The total plan is the result of everything you learn from the process, and the Executive Summary is the culmination of that full effort.

The Executive Summary is written last for the same reason that you do a full budget before you do the top pages. You may have a problem with this comparison if you do the top pages of the budget first or if you do only the top pages. At best, filling in numbers on the top pages is a "guesstimate." Only when you actually work out the real 20 to 30 pages of the budget, based on the storyboard breakdown, do you know the real costs.

Perhaps your guesstimate will end up being right on the mark. I don't think anyone has worked out the precise odds on that happening, but you might be more likely to win a lottery. A more probable scenario is that you will have backed yourself into a corner with original numbers that are too low. The real budget will turn out to be greater than your estimate by $500,000, $800,000, or even more. When that happens, your potential investors will be extremely unimpressed. If you are not sure how their money will be spent, ought they to trust you with it?

A business plan is the same situation magnified a thousand times. All the reasons outlined in the Introduction for writing a business plan come into play. You may be setting parameters for yourself that are unrealistic and that lock you into a plan you cannot carry out. In putting together the proposal, your investigation of the market may cause you to fine-tune your direction. Learning more about distribution—and we all can—may invite a reworking of your film release strategies.

Even if you were inventing a fictional company, as I did in the appendix, the Executive Summary must be written last. I did not know what I was going to say in the summary until the rest of the plan was written. Although I invented the company and statistics for the sake of example, my industry, market (except for the cats), distribution, and finance sections are all real. I did not know which facts about all those elements would apply to my particular situation. Likewise, until I worked out the numbers and cash flows, I could not summarize the need for cash.

(For cards outside the US please affix a postage stamp)

BUSINESS REPLY MAIL

FIRST CLASS MAIL   PERMIT NO. 78   WOBURN, MA

POSTAGE WILL BE PAID BY ADDRESSEE

DIRECT MAIL DEPARTMENT
BUTTERWORTH-HEINEMANN
225 WILDWOOD AVE
PO BOX 4500
WOBURN MA 01888-9930

At Butterworth-Heinemann, we are dedicated to providing you with quality service. So that we may keep you informed about titles relevant to your field of interest, please fill in the information below and return this postage-paid reply card. Thank you for your help, and we look forward to hearing from you!

What title have you purchased? └─┴─┘

Where was the purchase made? └─┴─┴─┴─┴─┴─┴─┴─┴─┴─┴─┴─┴─┴─┴─┴─┘

Name └─┴─┘

Job Title └─┴─┘

Institution └─┴─┴─┴─┴─┴─┴─┴─┴─┴─┴─┴─┴─┴─┴─┴─┴─┴─┴─┴─┘

Address └─┴─┘

Town/City └─┴─┴─┴─┴─┴─┴─┴─┴─┴─┴─┴─┴─┴─┴─┴─┴─┴─┴─┘

State/County └─┴─┴─┴─┴─┴─┴─┴─┴─┴─┴─┴─┴─┴─┴─┴─┴─┘

Zip/Postcode └─┴─┴─┴─┴─┴─┴─┴─┴─┴─┴─┴─┴─┴─┴─┴─┘

Country └─┴─┴─┴─┴─┴─┴─┴─┴─┴─┴─┴─┴─┴─┴─┴─┴─┴─┘

Telephone └─┴─┴─┴─┴─┴─┴─┴─┴─┴─┴─┴─┴─┴─┴─┴─┴─┘

email └─┴─┴─┴─┴─┴─┴─┴─┴─┴─┴─┴─┴─┴─┴─┴─┴─┴─┘

☐ Please keep me informed about other books and information services on this and related subjects.

(FOR OFFICE USE ONLY)

BUTTERWORTH-HEINEMANN IS ON THE WEB – http://www.bh.com/

US1

US1

The most difficult task for many entrepreneurs is resisting the impulse to write five quick pages and run it up the flagpole to see if anyone salutes. A business plan is not a script, and you cannot get away with handing in only a treatment. You must have your business plan well thought out, and you must present a complete package. Think of this as a rule. Other things are suggestions that you would be wise to follow, but this is definitely a rule. Go through the process first. By the time you have carefully crafted this document and gone through all the steps outlined in the book, you will be able to proceed with as few hitches as possible.

Presumably, you want to start a company that will last. It ought to be a cautious decision, not a haphazard one. You want to be sure that this business makes sense; you want to be able to meet any goals or verify any facts that you set forth. Passion does count. The film business is too hard and it takes too long to tackle projects if you do not have the passion for filmmaking. However, business facts are the glue that holds everything together in a tidy package.

Investors are the second reason that you write the Executive Summary only after you have carefully devised your business plan. Before you approach any money source, you want to be sure that your projected company makes sense. Potential investors did not accumulate their money by chance, and they are not likely to give you money on a whim. If you appear rash and impulsive, your 15 minutes of fame will run out before you know it.

Once in a while, there is that exception to the rule. Someone will ask to see just the Executive Summary. However, five will get you ten that the next communication says, "Let me see the rest of the plan." That person means today—now. He assumes that there is a body of work supporting your summary. You do not want to have to tell potential investors that you will have the complete plan in a month. You will lose their trust. The same is true if you need to put together a business plan for a single film—and it does happen. Certain investors or equity groups will ask for a business plan. Have all the market explanations, facts, and figures at hand and in order.

STYLE OF THE EXECUTIVE SUMMARY

The image experts say that you have 30 seconds to make an impression, whether it is at a job interview, in a negotiation, or at your local party place on a Friday night. Your business plan has the same amount of time. First impressions count; they will make the reader either want to read further or want to toss the proposal aside.

Cicero said that brevity is the charm of eloquence; this thought is good to keep in mind. In a few paragraphs, you must summarize the entire business plan to show the goals driving the business, the principal products, the essential market and distribution factors, and the major elements for the success of the business. Each of the chapters in the outline has its own summary. I know that it is hard to understand this repetition; students and clients ask about it all the time. That is why I keep coming back to it.

Earlier I said that the Executive Summary is the hook; you can also think of it as the bait that attracts the fish. You want the reader to be intrigued enough to read on. You need not try to rival John Grisham or Stephen King as a writer of mystery and suspense. You should not expect to keep anyone on the edge of the seat.

Simply tell the salient points in the Executive Summary. Less is more. If the Executive Summary of your plan is as long as this chapter, it is entirely too long. You can be long-winded later. All you want to do in this section is give your readers the facts with as little embellishment as possible. Remember that this is a business proposal, not a script.

LAYING OUT THE EXECUTIVE SUMMARY

Follow your outline when writing the Executive Summary. Give the basic information of each section with as little imagination as possible. Do not deviate from the path that you have already chosen. Anything you say here has to appear in more detail somewhere else in the proposal. Refer to the Executive Summary of the sample business plan (in the appendix) while reviewing how to lay out your own summary.

Overview

Typically, the first of the seven sections of the Executive Summary is called "Overview." However, you can call it "The Company" or "Overview of the Company" if you prefer. This section is the introduction to your business plan. It describes the outstanding elements of your goals and plans. From this section in our sample, readers know that the fictional company CCFI is passionate about cats and is devoted to making films about them. They also know how many films are planned, at what budgets, and over what period of time.

The Management Team

Although part of the company section, a mention of your management team should be added to the Executive Summary to give investors an idea of your team's experience and expertise. If you happen to be starting a company with a very well-known person, you will want to put his or her name up front on the first page. The names do not have to be well known; however, be sure not to name anyone who has not agreed to be part of the company.

The Products

In this section, give readers only the most important information about your proposed films. The synopses of your stories come later. In the sample business plan, I have noted that the planned films are related to a series of cat books and have suggested the tone of the stories.

The Industry

Before describing your specific segment of the marketplace, it is necessary to give an overview of the industry. Just a short paragraph to show the current shape and financial growth of the industry will do. For example, the current strength of independent films within the business as a whole is a point that you want to make up front.

The Market

In this section, you should give readers a feel for the markets for your product. I have made the market section of the sample plan a little longer than usual to explain the reasoning behind CCFI's plan. Because these films are a little unusual, I have spelled out their target markets.

You may have more than one product. In that case, you should devote at least one paragraph to each one. Readers know that all the necessary details will come later. You can even provide an index so that they can thumb right to the pages of interest.

Distribution

This part of the Executive Summary deserves some detail. Simply saying, "We will get distribution" is not enough. In the sample business plan, I felt it was necessary to explain why I would head to specialty theaters first. For this example, I assumed that no distributor was interested in CCFI's projects yet.

If you have distribution attached, give names here. Don't be shy. However, do be circumspect, as with the body of the plan. Only mention real companies from whom you have received actual written commitments. Phrases such as "We have interest from many companies to distribute our product" are public relations jargon. If potential investors think that they will find such meaningless generalizations in the rest of the plan, they may not read on.

If you are planning to self-distribute your product, mention it here. Hiding that fact until readers have worked their way through 20 pages of the business plan will not help you at all. State your reasons and describe in a few sentences your knowledge in the area of distribution.

Investment Opportunity and Financial Highlights

This section summarizes all the financial information in your plan. The first item to include is that all-important fact that hundreds of people leave out of their plans—how much money you want. Do not keep it a secret. The whole point of handing this plan to potential investors is to relieve them of a little of the green stuff. They know that; they just want to know how much.

Follow the amount with a summary of the profit and loss over the next five years to give readers an idea of when they will get their investment back. In the sample plan, the film with the biggest budget is being made near the end of the plan's forecast period (five years), so I have also stated the large revenue return to cover that investment. Even though the following years do not appear in the table, I calculated the returns in order to specify them here. Otherwise, it looks as if CCFI is going to lose a lot of money down the road.

Notice that I continually use the words *projection, forecast,* and *estimate* throughout the financial sections. Always qualify any expressions of future gain with one of these three words.

NEGOTIATION STANCES

The first strategy that I suggest in negotiating with an investor is to leave the subject out of this document altogether. By doing so, you keep the subject open for the real thing. Notice that the financial examples in the sample plan do not show a breakdown for the split with investors. They simply show the pretax dollars available for sharing. How the interested parties decide on equitable shares will depend on the number of parties involved, the type of entities involved, and proposals not foreseen by this plan. Many independent filmmakers involve their attorneys in these negotiations. Omitting specifics in the business plan gives your attorney more latitude in which to work.

I advise my clients to hold their cards close to the vest and to let the other person go first. Even though you have determined your needs and expectations in advance, a situation may arise that you had not anticipated. For example, one group that I worked with assumed in advance that they were looking for an investor in the company as a whole. I convinced them to forego detailing this investment share in the document. At the beginning, equity investors for the whole amount were hard to find, but the filmmakers knew several people who would invest in individual films. This option was better for them in the end. They kept control of the company, as there were no new partners, and they found the resources for financing features on an individual basis.

The Investor Wants How Much?

It is always perplexing for creative people who have put their hearts and souls into a project to give away 50 percent or more to an investor. A common complaint is, "I'm doing all the work. Why should he get 50 percent?" Your decision has to be based on whether the amount of investment money is worth giving the investor that large a share of the profits. I cannot solve this question for you. Your priorities and goals are part of this decision.

A standard business plan ploy that seldom gets funded is the 70/30 or 60/40 split in your favor. There may be someone out there willing to take it—never say never—but chances are that you will give your business plan to a variety of people, so reserve the bargaining for the individual. If potential investors seem unsophisticated, you can try it. If you are lucky, they will only laugh. If you are unlucky, they will laugh while leaving the room. At least the thought is not written in stone in your Executive Summary.

Specialized Financial Instruments

If your company is a limited partnership, private placement, or limited liability company, the amount of ownership is set ahead of time in the prospectus. Many entrepreneurs think that the business plan and the prospectus are one and the same. The prospectus includes a business plan, but also much more. It is a registration statement document that has been worked on carefully by an attorney. It includes securities that are to be sold, arrangements for selling, discounts and commissions to dealers, subscription agreements, how monies are to be distributed, and responsibilities and rights of company management and investors. An attorney must do the customary legal explanations. Otherwise, you run the risk of unintentionally opening yourself to accusations of fraud.

Even if you plan to use one of these business structures, I would keep the business plan a freestanding document. The business plan is part of the total package. Even though you want to do one of these financial structures, being able to circulate the plan separately could come in handy. You never know what opportunities may come your way.

2

The Company

Mere money-making has never been my goal.

JOHN D. ROCKEFELLER
Quoted in Study in Power (Allen Nevins)

STARTING IS EASY

There is a Chinese proverb that says, "To open a business is very easy; to keep it open is very difficult." To start a business, all you have to do is choose a name and have a phone; ergo, you are in business. To be successful, though, a business involves much more.

A company, according to the *American College Dictionary*, is "a number of people united for a joint action . . . a band, party or troop of people." For many filmmakers, this is a contradiction in terms. The lone screenwriter or director is an island of self-absorption; the filmmaker is king—long live the king! Running a business, however, embodies a totally different set of skills. It is a special kind of collaboration in which dictatorship does not work. For a business to run successfully, everyone must agree on its purpose, direction, and method of operation. This goal requires a lot of planning and communication.

At my first seminar, I started the day with a discourse on "Common Blunders in Business Planning." At the break, my assistant overheard someone say, "What is all this esoteric nonsense? We came here to find out where the investors are." Obviously, I had to find a way to make my meaning clear.

To start the next seminar, before even introducing myself, I put the following list of companies on the board:

- Vestron
- MCEG
- Weintraub Entertainment
- The Mount Company
- DeLaurentiis Entertainment
- Cannon
- Hemdale Film Corp.
- Avenue Entertainment
- Don Bluth Entertainment
- Intercontinental Releasing
- Aries Film Releasing
- Orion

I asked the seminar participants to tell me what these companies have in common. After attempts by several others, one attendee finally recognized that they all had declared Chapter 11 (bankruptcy with reorganization of the business) or Chapter 7 (bankruptcy with liquidation of the business). Some, such as Orion, have managed to recover from Chapter 11 and begin operating again; others have not. And in the last two years, Carolco and Cinergi have both gone out of business.

The first reaction from independent producers was that these companies were all big and that somehow their size contributed to their downfall. In reality, the reason companies—whether big or small—fail is the same in either case: lack of planning. Anyone can have bad luck. Part of planning, however, is looking at the future result of current decisions. In doing this, you can build in ways of dealing with bad luck and other problems. Granted, some crises are beyond your control. A bank failure or the bankruptcy of a distributor, for example, is such an outside event.

The business plan diagrams a path for you to follow. Along the way, there may be forks in the road and new paths to take. Flexibility in adjusting to such changing conditions is the key. On the other hand, taking every highway and byway that you see might take you in circles. In that case, you will never get a project completed and in the theaters. A balance is needed, therefore, between flexibility and rigidity. Planning provides this balance.

KNOW YOURSELF FIRST

When asked what they want to do, many filmmakers (or entrepreneurs of any stripe) reply either "I want to make money" or "I want to make films." There is nothing intrinsically wrong with either answer, but there are more questions to be considered. For example, what is the nature of the films you will make? What you are willing to do for money? And, ultimately, who are you?

Before characterizing your company for yourself or anyone else, make sure that you really know yourself. For example, one filmmaker told me that she intended to live and work in Georgia; she would make her films there and seek all money there. For her, this goal was nonnegotiable. This position may seem rigid to some people, but you have to know the lines you are not willing to cross.

Goals 101

Having and keeping a clear vision is important; it is as easy or as hard as you want to make it. Ensuring that you understand what you are truly about is the first step.

A full course in Goals 101 would be too long to include here, but let's have a quick review of the basic principles with a minimum of academic jargon. Setting goals merely means clearly stating your main purpose. Objectives are often shorter-term accomplishments aimed at helping you meet your main goal. For example, writing this book was my ultimate goal; teaching university classes was a short-term objective to help me reach my goal. Let me explain. I felt that the best way to establish credibility for a book contract was by teaching at UCLA. From the beginning, I knew that the pay would be low compared to consulting and other work; however, over the short term, the book was more important. Teaching at UCLA, then, became a greater priority than making lots of money.

Both aspects of your life may mesh quite well. Any conflicts need to be reconciled at the beginning. Otherwise, any conflicts between your business and personal aspirations may interfere with your success in one or both areas. Covert agendas are sometimes good to use with competitors, but fooling yourself is downright dangerous.

Formulating Your Goals

Formulating your goals may seem complicated, but it involves just two simple but essential steps:

1. Take a meeting with yourself at the start. (In Los Angeles and New York, everyone "does lunch.") Think about your plans, look at them, dream about them; then set out to test them against reality.
2. Write your plans down. Entrepreneurs love to declare that they can keep everything in their heads and do not have to write anything down. Big mistake! If your ideas are so clear, it will take you only a few minutes to commit them to paper. Anything you cannot explain clearly and concisely to yourself will not be clear to someone else. Writing down your goals allows you to see the target you are trying to hit. Then you can establish intermediate objectives or a realistic plan to accomplish these goals.

A word about money is in order. Heed what John D. Rockefeller said about money-making never having been his goal; other successful executives have made similar statements. Many talk shows have brought together groups of entrepreneurs to find out what motivates them. To a person, they always identify making the product, negotiating the deal, or some other activity as their main motivation; the money followed when they did the things they liked.

You usually accumulate money when you do something that you enjoy, that you are passionate about, and that you are good at. Many popular books have been written on this subject lately. I cannot stress too often that film is not an easy business. Be sure that it is the filmmaking that draws you—not just the tinsel and glitter.

Personal Goals versus Business Goals

Finding fulfillment is an elusive goal. To start, you must list and prioritize your goals. Unless you know where you are heading, you will be severely hampered in making decisions as you tread on down your path. People have both business and personal goals, so it is crucial to look at both categories.

First, take a look at your personal goals to make sure that you do not inadvertently overlook something you want. Your personal goals are your private desires, your plans about your lifestyle, the dreams that will bring a feeling of satisfaction outside of work. Can you identify your personal goals? What is important to you? Is it family? Church? Environmental issues? Riding horses in Montana? Consider the pursuits and activities that you find meaningful. Decide which are important enough to leave time for outside of pursuing your business.

If the idea of personal objectives still perplexes you, take some time to think about it. Being passionate about film is one thing; having nothing else in your life is something else. Once you can identify your personal goals, continue on.

List your personal goals on a piece of paper, not in your head; writing in the margins of this book is permitted. Describe as many or as few goals as you want, as long as you have at least one. Here are some examples to help you get started:

1. Improving my standard of living
2. Living in Albuquerque, New Mexico
3. Working out with a fitness trainer on a regular basis
4. Spending time with my family

Now identify your business goals. Again, make a list using the following examples as a guide:

1. Making environmental films
2. Making low-budget action/adventure films
3. Winning an Academy Award
4. Creating a distribution company in four years

On another piece of paper, list both the personal goals and the business goals side by side; then rank them in order, with 1 representing the most important to you. Only you can set these priorities; there is no right or wrong way to do it. Once you have made the two lists, compare them. What conflicts do you see? How can you reconcile them? Accomplish this task, and you will be ready to write the story of your business.

GETTING IT ALL TOGETHER

Putting together the story (or script) of your company is like making a pitch to a studio or writing a *TV Guide* logline—only longer. You want to convince an unknown someone of the following: (1) You know exactly what you are going to do, (2) you are creating a marketable product, and (3) you have the ability to carry it off. Essentially, you are presenting the basic "plot" of your firm. The difference is that a script provides conflicts and resolutions as plot points. By going through the previous writing exercise, you should have resolved any conflicts. "Just the facts, ma'am," as Sergeant Joe Friday would say.

Remember what your teacher taught you in high school English: who, what, when, where, why, and how. These questions are your guidelines for formatting the company section of your business plan. Before you go any farther, ponder these questions:

- Who are you?
- What films or other projects will you make?
- When will you get this show on the road?
- Where are your markets?
- Why are you making films?
- How are you going to accomplish everything?

Note that we are going to change the standard order a bit. The *why* needs to come at the beginning to set the scene for the rest of the story.

Why?—The Opening Pitch

Now that you have listed your personal and business goals, you can identify the underlying aim of the company, known in corporate circles as the mission statement. This statement describes your company's reasons for existence to you, your partners and managers, your employees, and, most of all, your money sources. It allows those marching forward with you to know whether you are all marching to the same drummer.

In the introduction to this chapter, I noted that one reason for company failure is lack of agreement on where the company is headed. A company is always a group project; there is far too much to accomplish for one person to do everything. The important thing is to ensure that company personnel do not go off in three or four different directions. Many companies that fail do so from lack of focus; you do not have to be one of them.

Do you have a specific philosophy? What do you want to do? Make the greatest films ever made? Make children's films? Make educational videos? Clearly define your philosophy for yourself and others. As long as people can identify with where you are heading, they will not get lost along the way.

When your philosophy or major goal is on paper, stand aside and take an objective look. Does this sound doable to you? Would it sound reasonable if someone else presented it to you? Most of all, would you take money out of your own pocket for it?

By the way, in writing up this description, you are not required to incorporate all your goals for the world to see. Your personal goals are yours alone—unless they affect the company significantly. Suppose, for example, that you are active in animal rights organizations. For that reason, you are adamant that no animals ever appear in your films. Everyone has the right to know about this dictum. It may affect scripts that have even innocuous animal scenes. Investors need to know about any major restrictions on your projects.

I am often approached by producers who have strong feelings about the source of investment money (how it was earned) or about certain countries to which they refuse to distribute their films. These countries always end up being major markets, so this credo strongly affects the company's potential revenue. Distributors do not like to give up lucrative markets, and investors do not like to give up potential profits. You have a right to your principles; just let people know what they are.

This brings us to a brief discussion about honesty. What if you intend to make, say, environmental films but fear that you will lose potential investors by being explicit? Should you keep your true plans to yourself? Should you claim to be making some other type of film, say, action/adventure? This question has come up in seminars and classes repeatedly. In one class, the following conversation took place:

STUDENT: If I tell them that I'm going to make environmental films, they won't give me the money.
L.L.: What are you going to tell them?
STUDENT: I won't tell them what kind of films I plan to make.
L.L.: You have to tell them something. No one is going to buy a pig in a poke.
STUDENT: I'll tell them that I'm going to make action films. Those always sell well.
L.L.: Then you would be lying to your own investors.
STUDENT: So? The idea is to get the money, isn't it?

L.L.: If lying doesn't bother you, how about fraud? The best case is
they will take their money back. At the very worst, you can be
liable for criminal penalties.
STUDENT: So?

You may think that I invented this conversation to make a point.
I wish that I had. Unfortunately, it is a true story. Is it surprising that
the university offered an ethics course, and no one signed up for it?
My job is not to lecture anyone, although it is tempting. Your moral
values are your own. Let it suffice to say that fraud is not a good
offense to commit, and most investors do not respond well to it.

Who?

By this time, you ought to know who you are, both personally and
professionally. Now you can use the mission statement to define your
company. Start the Company section of your business plan with a
short statement that introduces the company. Give its history, ownership structure, and details of origin. Include the following in the
statement:

1. Type of company
   Public or privately held
   Sole proprietor
   Partnership (general or limited)
   Corporation (type)
   State and city origin

2. Names of principals
   Owners
   Silent and/or active partners
   Officers

A beginning statement might be something like this:

> *AAA Productions is a newly formed California corporation whose officers are ,*
> *, and . Our principal purpose is the development and production of Hispanic-*
> *theme films as well as the employment of Hispanic cast in primary roles.*
>   *Over the next four years, the company plans to produce three indepen-*
> *dently financed feature films. During recent years, the movie market has*
> *become more open to stories about ethnic groups. Films with Hispanic themes*

have led the way and proved that there is a market. We feel that the time is right and that the window of opportunity is open for low- to medium-budgeted motion pictures.

Not only has the writer said what films the company intends to make, but he or she has also identified a specific goal that is both professional and personal. The company's "principal purpose" describes its mission statement. It is closely tied to the personal beliefs and desires of members of the company. To make it more complete, the writer might also define what size budget he or she considers to be "low" or "medium."

What?

Mysteries do not work, except in scripts. The readers of your business plan want a straightforward summary of your intentions. To say that you will make films or videos or whatever is not enough. What type of projects do you plan to do? In the Company section of the business plan, include a short recap of the projects you have planned. You will explain the individual projects in more detail later in the product section. You should summarize all the areas and industries that your plan covers, such as the following:

1. Films, videos, television movies of the week (MOWs), multimedia projects, industrials
2. Budgets of planned projects
3. Number of projects over a particular period of time
4. Type of functions (development, production, distribution) in which the company will be involved

Rationality must intercede here. What you want to do and what you are most likely to get done may be two different things. In one business plan in my office pile, for example, a group stated that it planned to make 10 to 12 feature films a year with average budgets between $8 and $15 million. This undertaking is laudable for a major studio, but it may be questionable for even a large independent production company because of the quantity of resources—both money and people—involved. For this brand-new company, it was a foolish goal. No one in the company had ever made a film before. Even if someone had, consider the effort. The films would require more than $100 million in production costs alone in the first year, not to say anything about finding the staff and cast to make them. Is this an investment that you would view as "reasonable" for your hard-earned money?

Nothing is ever absolutely impossible. People beat the odds every day. If entrepreneurs believed in the word "impossible," there would be no progress in the world. Nevertheless, you should weigh the scope of your venture against the experience of the people involved in it. If no one in your company has ever made a film, the odds are against your getting money for high budgets and multiple films per year. Aiming to produce one low-budget film the first year makes those odds a little better.

Experience producing or directing television programs, commercials, documentaries, and industrials is better than no experience at all; however, feature films are different in terms of time and budget. Being circumspect about the size of the feature budget in relation to your experience will not only impress investors but will also keep you from overextending your abilities.

Because starting a company implies that you plan to be in operation for at least five years, you must consider what your company will be five years hence. Analyze everything you plan to be doing over that time. If you plan to go into book publishing in year four, that goal needs to be part of your plan. Even plans to sell the company in five years must be mentioned. All of this is part of your projected bottom line. Although you may not know all the specifics, the size, scope, and type of your planned projects need to be stated.

Even if your company has been in business for a long time or the principals have considerable experience, never assume that readers have an intimate knowledge of your business. If your genre is horror, for example, you might write something like this:

> *We plan to produce horror films that are similar to* Nightmare *on Elm Street, except that Freddy Krueger has a love interest. We feel that the genre, which has been out of fashion, is due to make a comeback.*

The thought of Freddy being in love is horrible in and of itself, but you may find some passionate horror fan out there who wants to finance you. Put in a line or two about the current status of horror films, and show the success of the first *Nightmare on Elm Street* as a lower-budget film.

Do not go into exhaustive detail. You will do that later. Remember that it is important in this document to keep the malarkey factor to a minimum. That does not mean that you cannot put in a little public relations, but leave your press clippings for the appendix.

When?

In describing the company, you may have already stated how and when you began functioning as a company. You may have a great deal more to say, however. The majority of companies run by independent filmmakers are start-ups. If your company has only just begun, there may be a limited amount of information to state. Be clear about the current situation, whatever it is. You may still be someone else's employee, for example. But be sure that you really are in business or ready to launch. Go ahead and file forms that may be necessary for the type of company, print business cards, and have an address (even if it is your home or a post office box).

Starting Steps

You have already taken the first step of starting a business—translating the entrepreneur's vision into a concrete plan of choice. Next comes the practical process of actually setting up shop. You must create all those minutiae that say to prospective investors, "These people are really a going concern." Note the following checklist:

- Define the job descriptions of management.
- Determine the location and cost of offices.
- Have your stationery and business cards printed.
- Set up phones and a fax machine for easy communication.
- Arrange for professional guidance from an attorney and an accountant.
- Set up a checking account, and introduce yourself to your banker.

A more important step is choosing your legal form of business. There is no one form that is best for everyone. When making this decision, consult with your attorney or accountant. The most common forms of business are the following:

1. A *partnership* is a business with two or more co-owners. It can be established with a fictitious business name.
2. A *corporation* is a separate entity apart from its owners. To establish a corporation, you must file papers with the state and pay an incorporation fee. The business's assets and liabilities are separate from those of its owners. For this reason,

many people keep copyrights under their own names. Then, if the corporation goes kaput, you still own the films, the company name, whatever.

3. A *Subchapter S corporation* has a limited number of shareholders and certain tax benefits that differ from those for a general corporation.

4. A *sole proprietorship* is owned by one person. It is easy to initiate and faces little regulation. The individual owner has all the control but all the responsibility as well. It is the normal state of doing business for consultants and others who mostly work alone.

If the formation of your business is dependent on raising money, be clear about this. Just be sure that you will be in a position and willing to give full attention to the company on receipt of the money. It is critical to show some preparation (this business plan is an example) before seeking investors.

Suppose you own a company that has had problems in the past. Don't be coy. Obviously, you need other people's money for some reason. Most investors will insist on full disclosure. They need to know the depth of the problems to overcome. If you have leftover equity owners from a previous incarnation or have imprudently spent money on cars, confess now. In the business plan, the sin of omission is as serious as the sin of commission.

You may find yourself in another situation. What if the company was in some other line of business before you bought it? The name is established, but the business has not yet functioned as an entertainment entity. On the other hand, you may have bought an operating film company that has been unsuccessful. Both circumstances add assets and credibility to your company. However, do not attempt to give the impression that the company was anything other than it actually was or that it has made more money than it actually has.

Do not be afraid to state the facts. If a company made garbage cans before you bought it, say so. Investors want to know what they are getting into. Besides, being candid has its own rewards. People with money tend to know other people with money. Even if one prospect is not interested, his friend may be. So do not be afraid to tell him something he may not like. Eventually, he will find out anyway. You will lose not only an investor, but also the chance for him to recommend you to someone else. It is a small world, and the investing community is even smaller. Once you start getting a negative rap, it spreads quickly.

Where?

Potential investors want to know where you are going to sell your products and services. Although worldwide is a good thought, you should be more specific. If you are making your first independent film, it is not likely to have a $25-million budget. (If it does, please reconsider; you are not Miramax yet.) Let investors know if you expect distribution to take one or more of the following forms:

- Theatrical
- Specialty houses
- Ethnic communities
- Foreign markets
- Cable
- Direct-to-video

There are many options to choose from. Your choice may be complicated if you plan to produce more than one type of product and have different selling philosophies for each. Remember that this section is an introductory statement, not a thesis. A short summary, such as the following one, is all you need.

The company's objectives are to

1. Develop scripts with outside writers
2. Produce theatrical films with budgets from $1 to $5 million
3. Produce educational films for the health-care market
4. Make at least one movie directly for a cable network over the period
5. Explore overseas co-production and co-financing potential for the company
6. Distribute our films through independent distribution companies

How?

Up to this point, you have essentially outlined everything your company proposes to accomplish. In the rest of the plan, you will describe each step in detail. Chapter 3 is a continuation of the *what*. It is an in-depth study of each of your projects. Chapters 4 to 8 describe the *how*. This is the central plot of your business plan. How do you fit into the industry? How will you identify your place in the market? How do distribution and financing work, and how will you pursue each one?

MANAGEMENT AND ORGANIZATION

Conclude this section of your business plan with a brief description of the people involved in your company and the organization of the key team members. This means writing just a paragraph or two for each. Save the six- or seven-page résumés for the appendix. How much of the organization you describe depends on the strength of the management team.

Maybe you'll be lucky and have a well-known former studio executive as part of your company. Perhaps your executives have business expertise in some industry other than film. Film track records are important, but management experience in other industries also counts. If no one in your company has ever made a film, find someone who has and sign that person up. If you have no one currently, describe the job position and make the commitment to have it filled by the time your financing arrives.

Follow the example of a company with some entertainment experience:

> *The primary strength of any company is its management team.*
>
> *XXX's two principals have extensive business and entertainment industry experience.*
>
> *Ms. Simply Marvelous is XXX's president. Most recently, she has worked with MNY Co. in both acquisitions and production. Among the films that she was responsible for are* Cat Cries at Sunset, Phantom of La Loggia, *and* Dreaded Consultants IV. *Ms. Marvelous will have overall responsibility for the company's operations and will serve as executive producer.*
>
> *Ms. Freda Financial, vice president, brings to XXX varied business and entertainment experience, including five years' experience in motion picture finance with the Add 'Em Up accounting firm. Previously, Ms. Financial worked in corporate planning for the health-care industry.*

If you have a writer–director who has no feature film experience, you might write something like this:

> *Mr. Self Consumed will be writing and directing our first two films. Mr. Consumed has directed commercials for 15 years. In addition, he has done promotions for the Big Time cable system. Last year he directed the romantic comedy short film,* Louise Loves. *It was well received at several film festivals and won the critics' award at the Mainline Film Festival. His fifth feature screenplay is in development at Crazed Consultant Films.*

You should make these descriptions long enough to include the essential information, but the less important details should go elsewhere. For example, Mr. Consumed's commercials and the companies for whom he worked can be listed on a résumé in the appendix. For the sake of your reader's sanity, however, do not create a 10-page listing of all of a director's commercials, even in the appendix.

Catch 22—Experience

What do you do when no one in the company has any experience? Tread very carefully. My advice is to attach someone who does. Why would any investor believe that you can make a film with no previous experience and no help?

The amount of skill expected is related to the budget as well as the genre of the planned film. Suppose you have decided to make a $25-million film for your first venture. You have written a script and are partnered with people with no film experience. They have financial or retail backgrounds, but no direct knowledge of film. Would you take $25 million out of your own pocket for this?

In certain circumstances, you can use the ploy of discussing below-the-line attachments of merit. Some clients of mine, for example, happened to have an Academy Award–nominated and Emmy-winning cinematographer committed to their projects. It was to their benefit to include him in the organizational descriptions, as the partners' filmmaking backgrounds were not overpowering. The cinematographer can be of great benefit to the director, as all producers know.

Be careful how you do this, though. You want to avoid making the production of your films look like a committee effort. One wannabe producer came to me with a plan for a company, or at least a first movie, with himself as executive producer. He planned to start with a $20-million film and felt that running the computer system at a production company was appropriate film experience. His explanation read as follows:

> *Mr. So and So has 25 years' experience working with computer systems, 10 of them at X & X Production Company. Mr. So and So will be the executive producer on all films. He has an experienced crew ready to work with him. These technicians have a combined experience of 105 years in the film business. If Mr. So and So has any questions, they will be able to help him.*

This is a dangerous trap. Expecting that your inexperience will be covered by the experienced people working in various crew positions may backfire. The old saying "A camel is a horse designed by a committee" is applicable here. The producer is the manager of the business and must make the final decisions; therefore, the person in this position must have a foundation of knowledge on which to draw. Investors expect to see people in charge who have some vague idea of what they are doing.

When describing their experience, some people elaborate on the truth—to a fault. When applying for a job of any kind, it is frequently tempting to stretch your bio a bit, if not to make it up out of whole cloth. Think carefully before you do this. Filmmakers often put their most creative efforts into writing the management summaries. Compare this real biography to the "elaborated" version that follows:

Real biography

Leonard Levison has worked as an assistant to the associate producer on *The Bell Rings*. Before that, Mr. Levison was a production associate on four films at Gotham Studios. He began his film career as a script supervisor.

Business plan version

Leonard Levison produced the film, *The Bell Rings*. Prior to this project, he was co-producer on four films at Gotham Studios. He began his film career as an associate producer on various films.

"Exaggeration," you say? "Harmless public relations puffery," you add? This action is similar to the inflated income some people put down on a home loan application. You might assume that this is just the way things are done, but this action can come back to haunt you. A Los Angeles entertainment attorney told me about a court case in which the fictional management biographies of the filmmakers were the investor's sole reason for suing. He said that he "bet on people" and only read the management section of the plan.

Try to be objective about the company that you are creating. The likelihood that an investor will give money to totally inexperienced filmmakers is less than for a group with a track record. No situation, as I have said, is impossible. The safer you can make the downside (chance of losing money) for the investors, the likelier it is that they will write you a check. No matter how emotionally involved an individual investor might be in the project, there is usually an objective green-eyeshade type sitting nearby, trying to make your plan fit her idea of a "reasonable" investment.

A Word about Partnerships

In forming a company, you may want to take on one or more partners. The usual makeup is two or three people who co-own a company and work full time in it. Each one is personally liable for the others. It is quite common for good friends to become partners. Because of the relationship involved, many people in this situation often do not take the same care in doing business with friends that they would take with total strangers. No matter what the affinity for one another, agreements must be made and contracts signed. How many dear friends have you had at one time or another to whom you no longer speak?

A good partnership requires the presence of two contradictory elements. First, you and your partners must be very much alike so that your goals and objectives mesh. On the other hand, you must be very unlike and complementary in terms of expertise. Often, one partner is more cautious, the other more adventurous.

Whether to form a partnership can be a difficult decision. As in many other situations, the best step is to list on paper the advantages and disadvantages of partnership and see how it works out. The following are sample examples. First, the advantages:

1. I will have a measure of safety because it takes two to make any decision.
2. I will avoid the unremitting and lonely responsibility of doing everything by myself.
3. I will have a highly motivated co-worker, because she has a profit share in the company.
4. I will have knowledge and experience available to me that is different from my own.
5. I will have someone to share crises with.

Here are some reasons not to enter into a partnership:

1. The monetary rewards of ownership will be diluted.
2. I will not have total control.
3. I will have to share recognition at the Academy Awards.
4. My partner's poor judgment could hurt me and the company.
5. I will run the risk of a terrible falling-out with my partner.

LESS IS MORE

This section not only summarizes the essential facts about your company, but is an introduction to the rest of the business plan as well. It should be short and to the point. Prospective investors want to know the basics, which will be described in exhaustive detail throughout the rest of your proposal. Readers of the book's first edition, many of them writers, often have said that the phrase "less is more" was important to them. The following chapters will build on the foundation established here.

3

The Projects/Products

Why should people go out and pay money to see bad films,
when they can stay at home and see bad television for free?

SAMUEL GOLDWYN
Quoted in *The Observer*

PROJECT SCOPE

Theatrical films are the backbone of most filmmakers' business plans. As the industry changes, however, the potential for artistic expression is growing far beyond the notion of a single theatrical. In recent years, many filmmakers have successfully specialized in documentaries, commercials, industrials, educationals, or infomercials, as well as cable and video productions. Four years ago the future was CD-ROMs; however, that market seems to have dimmed. Now the industry looks to DVDs, the Internet, or CD-ROM played over the Internet as new outlets for film.

Whatever the projects or products, all business ventures in which your company will participate over the next five years should be addressed in this section of the business plan. This chapter demonstrates how to describe your projects. It explains not only the amount of information that you need to include, but also what you should leave out. This part of the business plan gives you the opportunity to expound on all of the projects that your company will pursue.

How do you know what you will be doing five years from now? Undoubtedly, you know more about some planned projects than about others; some of you may not even have specific projects yet. For example, you may have a script to shoot next year, but may not have a clue about the script for a film planned four years down the road. Nor can you know what delays may occur along the way. It is less important to be psychic than to be as accurate as possible in terms of intentions and timing. If circumstances alter the original plan, everyone involved will reevaluate it.

The Right to Know

As your partner, the investor has a right to know what activities are contemplated in order to make an informed decision. Several years ago, a young man came to me with a proposal to create a highly specialized series of films. He planned to sell them in a narrowly segmented market. The plan contained much discussion about the future success of his company, but the only description of the projects was the word "films." He cited an estimated population of millions that were going to see these unspecified films. Being the curious type, I asked him what kinds of films he planned to make. His answer was, "Good ones." I pressed on, trying to elicit more information. After all, he guaranteed that millions would clamor to see these films. He replied, "I'm not going to tell anybody anything. They might steal the idea. Besides, it's no one's business; all they need to know is that it's a good investment."

Don't laugh too loudly. This story is only one of many, and this young man's attitude is not unusual. "Films," as you may have realized by now, is not a sufficient description of your planned product. Putting yourself in the investor's shoes, how would this strike you? You would probably insist on knowing the content of these incredible films and how they were going to pay back your investment.

There are certainly a few real reasons that a filmmaker (or any other entrepreneur) might worry about revealing the details of a proposed project: (1) No identifiable plans exist, or (2) someone might steal the idea. Although theft of concept is not an unknown phenomenon, there is a difference between not telling the general public all about your plans and refusing to tell a potential money source. Prudent filmmakers refrain from describing script details in a loud voice at the local coffee shop or at a crowded party; they also resist the temptation to ask seven or eight friends to read their projects. However, the prudent *do* tell the right people enough information to prove the advisability of the investment.

Success in any business revolves around the product. In film, where all forward motion to the goal is content-driven, the story is crucial. To sell your projects, remember the refrain, "Story, story, story." Hype has a place also, but it must take a back seat in the context of this plan. The trick is to do some jazzy selling around a solid idea. All the public relations in the world will not save a bad film.

From Chapter 2, you know that the first goal for the business plan is to identify your future course of action. The second is to show investors how profitable your business will be. There is no way to forecast your success without specific ideas to evaluate. Does this mean that you must have all your scripts, directors, and stars in tow? Not necessarily, but you do need to have a framework. At the very least, for example, you want to know that you are going to produce X budgets and Y genres over Z period. You must provide enough information to estimate revenues and give the investor a fighting chance to agree or disagree with your forecast.

The Facts and Nothing But

Think of this section of the business plan as a story you are telling, with factual material as the priority. Fantasies may play an important part in scriptwriting, but using wish lists in this document can present a problem. Confusing the issue by citing a cast that has never heard of the project or books you do not own may give investors the wrong idea. Whether you create a false impression by accident or on purpose, the result is the same. Investors negotiate contracts based on the information you provide. In the end, if all is not as you indicated, promises can be canceled and money withdrawn.

FILMS

When describing your film projects, the objective is to present a descriptive overview of all the critical particulars without going into excessive detail. You should disclose each project's assets (components that may add commercial value to the project) as well as any nonmonetary values that are important to the type of films you want to make.

Show and Tell

The trick is to tell enough to engage readers, but not so much that you risk losing them. As we go through the different elements, we'll attempt to draw a line between sufficient content and excessive word-iness. Readers who must wade through pages of information that is hard to follow will just go to sleep.

Writers of scripts, books, and other literary pieces have a ten-dency when writing nonfiction to create a stream of consciousness that is hard to follow. Fiction requires emotional and subjective content that will draw readers into the fictional world. Business writing—and nonfiction of any kind—requires simplicity and directness. Dr. Linda Seger, noted author of books on screenwriting, says:

> *Screenwriting is about being indirect; proposal writing is about being direct. While the object of good fiction writing is to be subtle, hide exposition and present many ideas indirectly, good proposal writing insures that the audience is getting the information clearly and consciously.*

This is the reason why some genius invented the appendix. In the business plan, it contains details that may be outside the simple and direct information formula. As you proceed through the following sections, you will get a clearer picture of what this means. There are no official rules as to how much information you ought to include. You can do anything you want, but bring your common sense into play, and always try to be alert to the reader's point of view.

Scripts

Disclose enough material about each script so that readers understand its value. A short synopsis is the usual format. In a paragraph or two, you can tell the essentials of the story and indicate the genre of the film.

A student once questioned whether to include the title of his script. He feared that someone would steal it because it was inno-vative and catchy. Whether to reveal the film's title must be your decision. More often, writers fear that someone will pirate their ideas rather than their titles.

The first step to take to protect yourself from possible theft of concept or story is to copyright your project. Most writers register their scripts with the Writers Guild of America. An even better pro-cedure is to file for registration with the Library of Congress in Wash-ington, D.C. Once you have done this, you can prove that your story existed as of a particular date, and you can feel free to give it to others. Keep in mind that registration does not prevent theft; it just helps you prove ownership in the event of theft.

Keep your plot summary brief. The more complete plot treatment, which usually runs two to three typed pages, belongs in the appendix. If included in the body of the business plan, it will break the flow of the story you are trying to tell by taking the reader too far afield. If readers need more than the plot synopsis you provide, they will ask you for the treatment or for the complete script.

A reasonable plot summary might look like this:

Title: Boys Who Wreak Havoc

Four teenage boys decide to take over a small Wisconsin town. They kidnap the minister's daughter as a bargaining tool in their effort to make one of their members the mayor. Their attempt to control the population unites the townspeople, who, although previously selfish in their individual pursuits, come together to take back their town. The girl is saved without bloodshed, and peace reigns.

This paragraph tells enough about the story to give readers an idea of the type of film and the overall plot. It will be an action film (the title tells you that) with little violence ("without bloodshed"). Of course, the writer might have added a few more sentences to spell this out so that there would be no misunderstanding.

Include enough information to be sure that the reader does not misconstrue the type of film you plan to make. If the girl is raped or there is a nude scene, be sure to mention it. Failing to mention a scene that affects the nature of the film because you think potential investors might not like it is a sin of omission. It will be more than enough reason for your money source to take his money back, even after you have started production.

What if you do not have specific scripts? State this up front. Even without scripts in hand, you can define your projects in terms of size and genres. You may be looking for development money to obtain scripts or to live on while you write them. Concentrate on what you know about your project. You must tell investors at least the size of the films that you plan to make. One way to describe this situation is as follows:

We are planning to make three films with family themes over the next five years, ranging in size from $1 million to $10 million. The initial $50,000 will allow the company to develop scripts and to option stories from other writers. Production is expected to begin by the end of the first year after funding.

This scenario is not as tempting to investors as the first one, but it is doable. For investors, providing money for development is always a greater risk than providing money for well-planned projects. The danger for the investor is that the producer may never find the right project and begin production. However, if you have some experience and a credible team, you may be able to find development money.

What if you know neither the subject of your films nor the size of their budgets? In one plan, the company stated: "The producers plan to make low-budget features with the formula that has proved most profitable both in theatrical and video releases . . . scripts in this area are plentiful." Seems a little vague, doesn't it? Aren't you curious to know what these proven formulas are? Typically, the information in a proposal of this type is not enough. The right mix of ingredients is always a balancing act, but you probably would have to be a known filmmaker with an impressive track record to get away with this proposal. Even for an experienced moviemaker, this pitch would be hard to sell. Most people want to see specifics to which they can attach a value—either monetary or personal. Anyone with a modicum of business sense understands that handing out money to someone with no real plans except "to make a film" would appear to be foolish.

No doubt you can find an exception to this rule somewhere. Perhaps you've heard about an eager young filmmaker who, with his toothy smile and youthful enthusiasm, convinced a jaded deal-maker to hand over money. Nothing is impossible, but the odds are against this happening. This scenario sounds too much like a script and not enough like real life.

Another trap that filmmakers often fall into is represented by the following excerpt from another business plan: "The MNO Company hopes to make 10 to 12 feature films the first year, 10 to 12 the second year, and 15 to 20 films every year after that. Budgets will range from $15 million to $30 million." This program would be ambitious for an experienced producer at a major production company. Ten to 12 films a year is a studio schedule. Even five pictures in the first year for a moderately experienced filmmaker is a doubtful program. If your current objectives are similar, regroup and rethink.

At this point, you may also want to address the question of the potential audience for your flick. It does not hurt to add a qualifying sentence to your plot synopsis—for example, "Films about Wisconsin have grown in popularity recently, and we plan to capitalize on this phenomenon." However, save the discussion of the distribution and financial ramifications of your films for later sections. If your readers follow custom, they will have read the financial section before this one anyway. It is easiest for readers to follow your plan if you group all of the project descriptions together and do not digress to long discussions on other subjects.

ATTACHMENTS AND THEIR VALUE

In our balancing act, any person, place, or thing that adds value to the script is important. You want to give your project every chance to see the light of day, so recount any attachment with a perceptible value. Here are four examples of attachments: (1) options, (2) books, (3) stars, and (4) dollars. Keep in mind that your mother's opinion is not one of the choices.

Options

An option is a written agreement giving the producer exclusive rights to a project over some specific length of time. It ensures that no one else can make the project while the producer holds the option. Obviously, if you are the writer, it is your project. However, if you are representing other writers' scripts as part of your package, you must declare the ownership status. Representing films as your own when they are not is clearly a no-no.

Not only the script itself, but also the subject may need an option. If you are dealing with true stories of living people (or deceased persons whose estates own the representation of their likeness and life), you may need to seek permission to do the story. Getting the option, or "rights," after the fact can be a costly process. You do not want to be in the position of having a deal on the table for a film and going back to obtain the rights to it. After the fact, the subject can and often will deny having given verbal permission. If you have not done your homework, it is the subject's right to stop the production, which sometimes leads to an expensive payoff or a court injunction.

Books

A published book adds value to a film in several ways. The sales history adds clout to your project, the specialized market it represents provides a ready-made audience, and the book usually furnishes additional ways to hype the film. Unless it is your book and copyright, the first step is—you guessed it—an option. The cost of the option depends, again, on the person you are dealing with and the relative fame of the book. It would be useless to even try to give you prices. As soon as the ink is dry in this book, the market will have changed. In truth, a book option, like a script option, can cost anywhere from nothing to millions of dollars.

An author who has a subjective reason to want you to make the book into a film may be very generous in making an agreement with you. On the other hand, if money up front is the author's primary focus, he or she will drive as hard a bargain as possible. This area is one of the few in which your sparkling manner can have a concrete impact. Deals have been done, on occasion, because the author liked the filmmaker and wanted to see the project get made. Passion for the project counts for a lot in negotiating with authors. One way to be sure that you cannot use the book, however, is to refrain from seeking the rights to it.

Options can be gotten at a reasonable price if the timing and people involved are right. Two producers bought the rights for a paperback mystery book plus the author's next two books for a few thousand dollars. No one else had approached the author, and the books were not the type to make the best-seller lists. Nevertheless, the author had a large audience among mystery fans. With no competitive bidders, the producers were able to make a good deal.

Another producer optioned several books based on lesbian themes. The books had a large following, but the subject was still taboo at major studios. She was able to obtain a three-year option before the release of such films as *My Own Private Idaho* and *Fried Green Tomatoes*. These and other films that followed showed that themes about alternative lifestyles would not keep people out of the theaters. A change in the attitude of the trend-makers (studio executives, agents, and critics) increased the value of the producer's optioned books immediately.

Being able to read manuscripts before they are published gives you an advantage over other filmmakers. Agents have access to unpublished manuscripts all the time. If you happen to know about a book that is about to be published by an unknown author and you can strike a deal prior to publication, it may work to your advantage financially.

Stars and Other Fantasy People

Attaching star actors, star directors, and famous producers is the fantasy of many independent filmmakers. Having Brad Pitt or Tom

Hanks in your $500,000 film might be a recurrent dream of yours; but, unfortunately, their salaries have several more zeros. Nevertheless, you can have attachments that add value to your project.

At this level, we are clearly not thinking of "bankable" stars (the actors whose names ensure a certain level of box office when the film opens), but you still can have a name that interests an investor. The value of the name is often in the eye of the beholder. Foreign buyers often put value on names that are only so-so on a U.S. movie marquee.

Directors who command high salaries will also be out of the reach of very low-budget filmmakers. Emphasize your director's previous experience, but do not fabricate it. With higher budgets (over $5 million), the inexperience of the director becomes a bigger problem. Experienced actors are often unwilling to work with an unseasoned director, and investors become more nervous about spending their money.

Because the producer has the major responsibility for keeping the budget on track, previous experience with feature films is important. In independent filmmaking, the producer is often the only connection between investors and their money. Once the cash has gone into the film's bank account, investors must depend on the producer to protect its use. Not only does the producer watch the money, but she has to have enough clout with the director to stop him from going over budget. Always keep in mind that this process is a balancing act of all the different elements.

Money

"Well," you say, "of course, money adds value." It seems redundant but really is not. Clearly, hard cash for development and production has a straightforward relationship to your project, but what about any partial funds attached to your project? For some reason, newer producers do not think to mention them as part of their product description, but they should. If any money at all is attached to your project, announce it here. You will discuss it at greater length in the financial section. Remember that all attachments are part of the film's synopsis. You want to depict any ingredient of this mix that will positively influence someone to make your film. In addition to hard cash, you should mention any co-production agreements, below-the-line deals, negative pickups, or presales.

BUDGETS—THE SHORT FORM

For prospective investors to evaluate your films completely, they need to know the size of the budget. Again, we have two types of films: those with complete scripts and those that are just a gleam in the producer's eye. When real scripts exist, real budgets should exist also.

To save money, many filmmakers pass a tuning fork over their script and say, "One million dollars." Do not just make up a figure. Anyone who contemplates financing your film will take this number seriously. So should you.

Many independent films have been delayed because the money ran out during either principal photography or post-production. The investors have said, "You told me $800,000, so that is all you are getting." Studios often have reserves for a certain amount of budget overruns; equity investors do not.

Some filmmakers develop only the two top sheets of the budget—this is just one step ahead of the tuning fork method—and figure out the complete cost later. Do it now to save explanations later. Estimating the cost of the general categories (cast, location, wardrobe, and so on) can be very dangerous, no matter how experienced you are. Break down the script (production managers are good at this job) and calculate the entire amount.

In describing your product, you should simply state the size of the budget along with its attachments. A paragraph or two on the entire project will be sufficient. Consider the following example:

> *This film has a $2-million budget, based on filming in Cincinnati. Susie Starstruck and Norman Goodlooking are set to star in the film. Ms. Starstruck has been featured in* The Gangbusters *and* Return of the Moths. *Mr. Goodlooking has appeared in several movies of the week. Herman Tyrant, the director, has made two low-budget films (*Be My Love *and* Girls Don't Sing*) and has previous experience in commercials. The film has partial financing of $100,000 from an equity investor, with all territories still free for distribution.*

In this paragraph, the writer has explained the essentials. From the preceding paragraph, we have learned the basic plot of the film. Here we learn the size of the budget, the location (much of the cost in this example is predicated on the film being shot in a right-to-work state), and the experience of the lead actors and director. One investor already has an equity position, but all the sales markets are available. Note that the writer has saved any discussion on the implications of adding another equity investor for the finance section.

Do not worry about repetition; it is part of the building-block formula. You give an overview of the product. Then, in the distribution and finance sections, you go into greater detail about pertinent elements.

What if you do not have a full script or actors and have little or no experience? Do not lose heart. You can still explain what you are planning to do. Look at this example:

> *The ABC Company plans to make four films over the next five years. The first two films will be low-budget ($250,000 and $1 million, respectively) and will deal with coming-of-age themes. They are intended for distribution in specialty theaters. Both films are in the treatment stage, and the director, Fearless Author, will write the screenplays. Mr. Author wrote and directed four short films, two of which have won awards at film festivals. Mr. Experienced Producer, whose films include* Growing Up? *and* Life Is a Flower, *has given us a letter of intent agreeing to serve as executive producer.*
>
> *The third and fourth films will be in the $3- to $5-million range. Mr. New Producer will produce these films after serving as co-producer on the first two. Neither treatments nor scripts exist for the third and fourth films. They will be in development during the first two years.*

Common sense will tell you that this package has less substance than the one given above. It may be harder to find financing, but not impossible. If you find yourself in a similar situation, all you can do is try to create as many advantages for yourself as possible. The worst approach you can take is to say, "We are nobody with no plans. We plan to find no one experienced in anything, but we want your money anyway." It's true that no one is going to be this truthful, but on many proposals, it is not difficult to read these words between the lines. You have to learn to make realistic compromises to reach your goals.

Too Much Can Be Harmful

One of the biggest nightmares that financial folks have is to receive a 10-pound business plan that includes every piece of paper in the producer's desk. Your goal is to have people read your proposal; therefore, you want to give them enough information without making the plan too heavy to lift.

Suppose you have a complete budget for each of your projects. Do not put them anywhere in this business plan. An interested party will ask for them soon enough, and you can have the dubious thrill of explaining every last nickel. If you have a strong desire to show detail, you can put the top sheets of the budgets in your appendix for perusal at the reader's convenience.

The same goes for the biographies of the stars, director, producer, and anyone else involved with your projects. A few sentences describing each principal's background is sufficient. The three-page bios do not need to be in the body of the plan. If you feel strongly that someone will have a burning need for this information, the appendix is the place for it.

Don't make potential investors guess about the applicable credits by including newspaper reviews in your business plan. Summarize the essentials. If you are bursting at the seams with your wonderful reviews, you know where they go—the appendix. As far as I am concerned, photocopies of any kind should be forbidden by law to appear in business plans. When you are trying to separate investors from their money, a well-typed, neat page counts; it shows that you care enough to make some effort.

One plan in my possession actually weighs in at two pounds. Thrown in with the appropriate and readable text are nine pages detailing every industrial and commercial film that the director made. Later sections include photocopies of numerous tables and articles from various publications. The investor is presumably supposed to wade through all this paper and reach a conclusion. Not wise. By filling your plan with extraneous paper, you might appear to be covering up an absence of fact, or you might give the impression that you do not understand the proposal yourself. Personal impressions are intangible, but they count. Always keep in mind that the human beings who read your treatise will have human failings. Once they are distracted or annoyed, their attention may be lost, and your package may be tossed in the "forget it" pile. Some rules are made to be broken, but the one about brevity and clarity is not.

NONTHEATRICAL FILMS

Markets exist for nontheatrical documentaries, direct-to-video productions, educationals, industrials, and other types of nontheatrical films. These categories are not as lucrative as theatrical film and its attendant ancillaries (video, cable, and foreign markets, for example), but it is possible to make a career from them. The educational film market has its own circuit. Distributors who specialize in this area often pay the filmmaker a percentage of the grosses, resulting in a small profit. A successful background in this format can help your cause. Several groups of neophyte feature producers have strategies to begin their independent feature film careers with educational films geared for the medical market. These can be made at a low cost ($5,000 and up), the subject is the star, and the production period is extremely short. No attachments are required, but if a famous doctor wants to appear at a reasonable price, do not turn her down. As with other products, anything that increases the sales value brings in more money.

The production of films intended to go direct-to-video, skipping theatrical release, closely resembles all the standards for quality of attachments for theatrical films. The potential for making money with direct-to-video productions is different from that of theatrical films. The lure of a breakout box office success, such as *Dirty Dancing* or *The Crying Game*, does not exist, and there are no theatrical grosses to drive sales. However, a case can be made for lower marginal profits over a large number of films.

Companies that used to specialize in this area have begun to turn to feature production; in most cases, they have gone out of business. Investors may not be as plentiful, but they are out there somewhere. In the nineties, the video market has weakened, however. If you plan to start a company with this strategy, research your market first. There is no computerized database for these films, as data is usually only accumulated on films that have a theatrical opening. The main sources of information are the foreign buyers and distributors themselves.

Timing of These Products

Whether you are dealing with one product or several, being able to predict the sequence of events for production and sales has to be carefully charted over the next five years. Many companies are based on multiple products. Producers or their partners may come from other areas of the entertainment industry or from other businesses. It is not unusual for principals to use previously gained skills to start a company. In the case of multimedia, the producer may want to start with standard feature films and move into the new technology later on.

Whether the chicken or the egg comes first depends on your objectives. Each product has its own purpose and its own natural place in the five-year time line. The sequence of events, however, should have some meaning rather than be haphazard. Often, film-makers with backgrounds in documentaries, educational films, commercials, or industrials will start with those products to lay a financial groundwork for the company, then proceed to feature films two or three years down the road. The profits from these products can be used for part of the production cost of subsequent films, with the rest of the money being supplied from outside sources.

To launch any product takes thought and skill. If you can define the project, explain the market, and present logical financial information, you are on the right road. More often, producers with no experience in the nontheatrical field will add nontheatrical products to their business plan. For some reason, they assume that an inexpensive product resembling "real business" as compared to feature films is guaranteed to make money. They will explain this other endeavor with a simple statement, "This will bring a lot of money to the bottom line."

Any business that you enter into without enthusiasm or knowledge has built-in problems. Making a business successful is hard enough without the added burden of having no real interest in it. It requires extensive study to launch a product in any market. By the time you learn how a new business works, it may be too late for financial success. Rather than creating a miracle source of cash for films, you are likely to create huge debts. Worst of all, if you lose the initial funds, it may be difficult or impossible to raise more.

In combining different products along your five-year time line for the business plan, you want to keep in mind two questions:

1. How will these products work together?
2. What is the best use of the combined talents of the principals?

In one company that plans to begin with medical videos, one of the partners is a doctor. Her background as both a physician and a writer provides not only scripts for the videos but in-house quality control on accuracy. Presumably, she also knows the most efficient venues for distribution of the videos. This sounds good in concept. It is a smart move to go into a business in which you have previous work experience. However, the production of video differs from that of film in several important ways. It involves aspects of business not usually dealt with by producers, such as manufacturing, inventory control, warehousing, consumer advertising, and retail marketing and pricing.

Experienced business judgment helps. Running a commercial production company, for example, is different from being a producer or director at one. This type of company often has a chief executive and follows a typical bureaucratic structure with multiple vice presidents, similar to the structure of the studios. Rather than being involved in the creative side of the business, these executives keep all the business balls in the air and the profit margins on track.

Whether a product begins the company, is sold concurrently with other products, or appears by itself at a later time depends entirely on the overall picture. The critical element for your business plan is showing that you know how all the pieces fit together. Each project essentially has its own mini-plan, with an analysis of the market, the industry, and finances. When you fit all the projects together, you have the plan for the whole company. At the end of the day, there has to be one bottom line for the whole package.

ASSESSING STRENGTHS AND WEAKNESSES

Casting an unbiased eye over your plans is always hard for entrepreneurs. A strong desire for everything to work often clouds your vision. Evaluating the strengths and weaknesses of your project in the beginning, however, will save time, turmoil, and money later. You might be able to describe the strengths of your company as follows:

- Associates of the company possess unique skills or experience.
- The distinctive characteristics of our projects set them apart from our competitor's products.
- We have special relationships with distributors or other professionals or companies in related fields.
- There are other unique aspects of this business that will help us.

Film production companies are often started with a combination of production and distribution personnel with varying levels of experience. Newer filmmakers team with experienced hands-on producers outside the company. Well-established companies often seek experienced personnel when going into new lines of endeavor. New Line Cinema, for example, grew into a major independent production and distribution company with low-budget, mass-market products, such as the *Nightmare on Elm Street* films and *Teenage Mutant Ninja Turtles.* When the company created a division to emphasize high-quality specialty films, they hired an executive with comparable experience. Ira Deutchman, first president of Fine Line Features and currently president of Redeemable Films, had previously provided marketing services for such specialty films as *sex, lies, and videotape, To Sleep with Anger,* and *Metropolitan.* New Line recognized that this new niche market had its own production criteria and distribution techniques.

No major company has developed similarly since Propaganda, which was started in 1986 by Sigurjon Sighvatsson and Steve Golin, as a commercial and music video house. The company began to participate in specialty-type fare, such as *Wild At Heart, Red Rock West,* and *Canadian Bacon.* In 1992, Polygram, which had been a minor investor, purchased the company and it began to make more mass-appeal films, such as *Sleepers.* In 1994, Sighvatsson left the company to form Lakeshore Entertainment with Tom Rosenberg, formerly head of Beacon Communications, with the desire to focus more on content. Lakeshore has financed low- and medium-budget films (e.g., Tom DiCillo's *Box of Moonlight* at $5 million and *Til There Was You* at $18 million).

On the reverse side of the ledger are your company's weaknesses. Be honest with yourself when identifying your company's failings. This exercise saves many companies from later failure. By converting the strength statements to negative statements, you can spot problems. Write them down on a piece of paper to review:

- No one in this company possesses unique skills or experience.
- Our projects have no distinctive characteristics that set them apart from our competitors' products.
- We have no special relationships with distributors or other professionals in related fields.
- There are no other unique aspects of this business that will help us in any way.

Being good in one area of business does not guarantee success in another. For example, suppose an entrepreneur from one area of entertainment, such as commercials, decides to go into theatricals, an area in which he has no experience. Although he knows how to manage a profitable business, feature filmmaking has its own unique set of concerns. The business requires larger sums of money per project than do commercials and involves greater risks in terms of market. Commercials are done on order from a customer; feature films are made on speculation of finding a customer. In addition, designing a good commercial is not related to knowing what makes a good script. Successful executives often rush into new businesses without preparing properly. Used to calling all the shots, they may have trouble delegating authority or may hire lower-level development personnel rather than experienced producers in order to maintain control. The producer can counter these weaknesses by studying the new industry first and hiring seasoned film people.

Running through this exercise will help you in two ways. First, you will find out where the holes in the dike are so that you can plug them before any leaks occur. Second, you can use it to assess how much confidence you or anyone else can have in your organization. In addition, pointing out the obvious to readers never hurts. You should not make readers work to see the good points. As to weaknesses, most investors are sophisticated executives and will see the problems themselves. If you do not mention how you will overcome the obstacles your company faces, the investor may question your ability to understand them. Being frank may help your cause rather than hurt it.

4

The Industry

Once we get out of the '80s, the '90s are going to make the '60s look like the '50s.

DENNIS HOPPER TO KIEFER SUTHERLAND
in *Flashback*

With the exception of perhaps Thomas Alva Edison, no film entrepreneur has ever operated in a vacuum. Edison invented the first camera that would photograph moving images in the 1890s. Moving images had existed before. Shadows created by holding various types of objects (puppets, hands, carved models) before a light were produced on screens all over the world. This type of entertainment, which most likely originated in the Orient with puppets, was popular in Asia, Europe, and the United States. There are even reports of an early form of moving camera in Paris in the late 1800s. Then along came Edison with his kinetograph, and shortly thereafter, the motion picture industry was born.

Even Edison did not have a monopoly on moving pictures for long. Little theaters sprang up as soon as the technology appeared. In 1903, Edison exhibited the first narrative film, *The Great Train Robbery*. Seeing this film presumably inspired Carl Laemmle to open a nickelodeon, and thus the founder of Universal Studios became one of the first "independents" in the film business.

Edison and the equipment manufacturers banded together to control the patents that existed for photographing, developing, and printing movies. Laemmle decided to ignore them and go into independent production. After several long trials, Laemmle won the first movie industry antitrust suit and formed Independent Moving Pictures Company of America. He was one of several trailblazers who formed start-up companies that would eventually become major studios. As is true in many industries, the radical upstarts who brought change eventually became the conservative guardians of the status quo.

Looking at history is essential for putting your own company in perspective. Each industry has its own periods of growth, stagnation, and change. As this cycling occurs, companies move in and out of the system. Not much has changed since the early 1900s. Major studios are still trying to call the shots for the film industry, and thousands of small producers and directors are constantly swimming against the tide.

IDENTIFYING YOUR INDUSTRY SEGMENT

Industry analysis is important for two reasons. First, it tests your knowledge of how the system functions and operates. Second, it reassures potential partners and associates that you understand the environment within which the company must function. As noted, no company works in a vacuum. Each is part of a broader collection of companies, large and small, that make the same or similar products or deliver the same or similar services. The independent filmmaker (you) and the multinational conglomerate (most studios) operate in the same general ballpark.

Film production is somewhat different when looked at from the varied viewpoints of craftspeople, accountants, and producers. They are all part of the film industry, but they represent different aspects of it. Likewise, the sales specifications and methods for companies such as Panavision, which makes cameras, and Kodak, which makes film stock, are different, not only from each other, but also from the act of production. Clearly, you are not going to make a movie without cameras and film (or video), but these companies represent manufacturing concerns. Their business operations function in a dissimilar manner, therefore, from filmmaking itself.

When writing the industry section of your business plan, narrow your discussion of motion pictures to the process of producing and directing a film, and focus on the continuum from box office to the ancillary (secondary) markets. Within this framework, you must also differentiate among various types of movies. Making the $75 million *Independence Day* is not the same as producing a $450,000 film about a cat. A film that requires extensive computer-generated special effects is different from a film that just has a lot of computers in it. Each has specific production, marketing, and distribution challenges, and they have to be handled in different ways. Once you characterize the industry as a whole, you should discuss the area that applies specifically to your product.

In your discussion of the motion picture industry, remember that nontheatrical distribution—that is, pay-per-view, cable and domestic and foreign television, syndication and video—are part of the secondary revenue system for films. Each one is important enough to be an industry in itself. However, they affect your business plan in terms of their potential as a revenue source.

Suppose you plan to start a company that will supply product specifically for cable and pay-per-view, or you plan to mix these products with producing theatrical films. You will need to create separate industry descriptions for cable and pay-per-view. This book focuses on film, but the method is the same for these other areas; only the specific products are different.

If you are considering television, multimedia, or the Internet, you will be crossing industry lines. All are industries that behave differently from film and from each other. Whenever you are making products directly for another medium, such as movies-of the week, in addition to feature films, you must discuss the additional industry as well.

A LITTLE KNOWLEDGE CAN BE DANGEROUS

You can only guess what misinformation and false assumptions about the film industry the readers of your business plan will have. Just the words *film* and *marketing* create all sorts of images. Your prospective investors might be financial wizards who have made a ton of money in other businesses, but they will probably be uneducated in the finer workings of film production, distribution, and marketing. One of the biggest problems with new film investors, for example, is that they expect you to have a contract signed by the star or the actual completion bond guarantee in hand before financing. They do not know that the money must at least be in an escrow account before either of these contracts is generated. Therefore, it is necessary to take investors by the hand and explain the film business to them.

You must always assume that the investors have no previous knowledge of this industry. Things are changing and moving all the time, so you must take the time to be sure that everyone involved has the same facts. It is essential that your narrative show how the industry as a whole works, where you fit into that picture, and how the segment of independent film operates.

Even entrepreneurs with film backgrounds may need some help. People within the film business may know how one segment works but not another. As noted in Chapter 3, it can be tricky moving from a studio or large production company to an independent or specialty house. For all its strengths, the studio is still a protected environment. The precise job of a studio producer is quite simple: making the film. Other specialists within the studio system concentrate on the marketing, distribution, and overall financial strategies. Therefore, a producer working with a studio movie does not necessarily have to be concerned with the business of the industry as a whole.

Likewise, foreign entertainment and movie executives may also be naive about the ins and outs of the American film industry. The history of Sony Entertainment proves that. Some have hired consultants to do in-depth analyses of certain U.S. films in order to understand what box office and distribution mean in this country. My experience has shown that foreign executives know how the industry works in their own countries, but often are confused about how it functions in the United States. In Japan, for example, the typical production cost of a film is between $4 and $8 million. Although U.S. films score higher grosses there than Japanese films do (Fox's film *Independence Day* has grossed $40 million to date in Japan), Japanese films seldom reach that level.

As you go through this chapter, think about what your prospective investor wants to know. When you write your plan, answer the following questions:

- How does the film industry work?
- What is the future of the industry?
- What role will my company play in the industry?

The rest of this chapter compares studio and independent motion picture production. It also provides some general facts about production and exhibition.

MOTION PICTURE PRODUCTION AND THE STUDIOS

Originally, there were the "Big Six" studio dynasties: Warner Brothers, Twentieth Century Fox, Paramount, Universal, Metro-Goldwyn-

Mayer (MGM), and Columbia (now Sony Pictures Entertainment). After the Big Six came the Walt Disney Company. Together, these studios are referred to as "the Majors." Although the individual power of each has changed over the years (the most recent to experience these ups and downs was MGM), these studios still set the standard for the larger films.

Until the introduction and development of television for mass consumption in the fifties, these few studios were responsible for the largest segment of entertainment available to the public. The advent of another major medium changed the face of the industry and lessened the studios' grip on the entertainment market. At the same time, a series of Supreme Court decisions forced the studios to disengage from open ownership of movie theaters. The appearance of video in the seventies changed the balance once again.

How It Works

Today's motion picture industry is a constantly changing and multifaceted business that consists of two principal activities: production and distribution. Production, described in this section, involves the developing, financing, and making of motion pictures. Any overview of this complex process necessarily involves simplification. The following is a brief explanation of how the industry works.

The classic "studio" picture was defined as one costing more than $10 to $12 million. Now the threshold has moved, as foreign money has moved into bigger budgets. Over $15 million, however, most films need the backup a studio can give them. In addition, a studio is often in a better position to take a chance on a borderline film. It spreads its risk over 15 to 20 films. As long as the failures occur with the lower-budget films and the successes are with the higher-budget films, everyone is still in business.

The independent investor, on the other hand, has to sink or swim with just one film. It is certainly true that independently financed films made by experienced producers with budgets of more than $12 million are being bankrolled by production companies with consortiums of foreign investors, but for one entity to take that kind of risk on a single film is not the rule. Just to recoup the investment on even a $12 million film requires at least a $30-million box office. (Studios roughly estimate a break-even box office total by multiplying 2.5 times the production costs.)

At a studio, a film usually begins in one of two ways. The first method starts with a concept (story idea) from a studio executive, a known writer, or a producer who makes the well-known "30-second pitch." The concept goes into development, and the producers hire scriptwriters. Many executives prefer to work this way. In the second method, a script or book is presented to the studio by an agent or an attorney for the producer and put into development. The script is polished, and the budget determined. The nature of the deal that is made depends, of course, on the attachments that came with the concept or script. Note that the inception of development does not guarantee production, because the studio may have many projects on the lot at one time. A project may be changed significantly or even canceled during development.

The next step in the process is preproduction. If talent was not obtained during development, commitments are sought during preproduction. The process is usually more intensive because the project has probably been "greenlighted" (given permission to start production). The craftspeople (the below-the-line) are hired, and contracts are finalized and signed. Despite recent press reports to the contrary, producers do strive to have all their contracts in place before filming begins.

The filming of a motion picture, called "principal photography," takes from 8 to 12 weeks, although major cast members may not be used for the entire period. Once a film has reached this stage, the studio is unlikely to shut down the production. Even if the picture goes over budget, the studio will usually find a way to complete it. After principal photography, post-production begins. This period used to require 6 to 9 months but might be much shorter for some films today, thanks to recent technological developments.

Tracking the Studio Dollar

Revenues are derived from the exhibition of the film throughout the world in theaters and through various ancillary outlets. Studios have their own in-house marketing and distribution arms for the worldwide licensing of their products. Because all of the expenses of a film—development, preproduction, production, post-production, and distribution—are controlled by one corporate body, the accounting is extremely complex.

Much has been written about the pros and cons of nurturing a film through the studio system. From the standpoint of a profit participant, studio accounting is often a curious process. One producer has likened the process of studio filmmaking to taking a cab to work, letting it go, and having it come back at night with the meter still running. On the other hand, the studios make a big investment. They provide the money to make the film, and they naturally seek to maximize their return.

If your film is marketed and distributed by a studio, how much of each ticket sale can you expect to receive? Table 4.1 provides a general overview of what happens when a finished film is sent to an exhibitor. The table traces the $7.00 that a viewer pays to see a film. On average, half of that money stays with the theater owner, and half is returned to the distribution arm of the studio. It is possible for studios to get a better deal, but a 50 percent share is most common. The split is based on box office revenue only; the exhibitor keeps all the revenue from popcorn, candy, and soft drinks.

For all intents and purposes, the distribution division of a studio is treated like a separate company in terms of its handling of your film. You are charged a distribution fee, generally 30 to 40 percent, for the division's efforts in marketing the film. Because the studio controls the project, it decides the amount of this fee. In Table 4.1, the distribution fee is 30 percent of the studio's share of the ticket sale, or $1.05.

Next comes the hardest number to estimate. the film's share of the studio's overhead. "Overhead" is all of the studio's fixed costs—that is, the money the studio spends that is not directly chargeable to a particular film. The salaries for management, secretaries, commissary

Table 4.1 Tracking the Studio Dollar

Your Box Office Dollar	$7.00
Exhibitor Share (50%)	$3.50
Studio Share (50%)	$3.50
Studio Share (50%—see above)	$3.50
minus distribution fee (30% of $3.50)	1.05
	2.45
minus overhead fee (12% of the $3.50)	0.42
Amount left to apply toward film negative (58% of the $3.50)	$2.03
—does not include interest charges	

Note: This example is based on average results. An individual film may differ in actual percentages.

employees, maintenance staff, accountants, and all other employees who service the entire company are included in overhead. A percentage system (usually based on revenues) is used to determine a particular film's share of overhead expenses.

It should be noted that the studios did not make up this system; it is standard business practice. At all companies, the non-revenue-producing departments are costed against the revenue-producing departments, determining the profit line of individual divisions. A department's revenue is taken as a percentage of the total company revenue. That percentage is used to determine how much of the total overhead cost the individual department needs to absorb.

In Table 4.1, a fixed percentage is used to determine the overhead fee. Note that it is a percentage of the total rentals that come back to the studio. Thus, the 12 percent fee is taken on the $3.50, rather than on the amount left after the distribution fee has been subtracted. In other words, when it is useful, the distribution division is a separate company to which you are paying money. Using that logic, you should be charged 12 percent of $2.45, but, alas, it doesn't work that way.

Now you are down to a return of $2.03, or 58 percent of the original $3.50, to help pay off the negative cost. During the production, the studio treats the money spent on the negative cost as a loan and charges you bank rates for the money (prime rate plus one or two percentage points). That interest is added to the negative cost of your film, creating an additional amount above your negative cost to be paid before a positive net profit is reached.

We have yet to touch on the idea of stars and directors receiving gross points, a percentage of the studio's gross dollar (e.g., the $3.50 studio share of total box office dollar in Table 4.1). Even if the points are paid on "first dollar," the reference is only to studio share. With several gross point participants, it is not unusual for a well-grossing film to show a net loss for the bottom line.

Studio Pros and Cons

When deciding whether to be independent or to make a film within the studio system, the filmmaker has serious options to weigh. The studio provides an arena for healthy budgets and offers plenty of permanent in-house staff to use as a resource during the entire process, from development through post-production. Unless an extreme budget overrun occurs, the producer and director do not have to worry about running out of funds. In addition, the amount of product being produced at the studio gives the executives tremendous clout with agents and stars. The studio has a mass distribution system that is capable of putting a film into as many as 2,000 theaters on opening day if the budget and theme warrant it. Finally, the filmmaker need not know anything about business beyond the budget of the film. All the other business activities are conducted by experienced personnel at the studio.

On the other hand, the studio has total control over the film-making process. Should studio executives choose to exercise this option, they can fire anyone and hire anyone they wish. Once the screenplay enters the studio system, they can change it in any way, including altering the credits. The original screenwriters may not even see their names listed under that category on the screen. For example, the original co-writers of *The Last Action Hero* asked for an arbitration hearing with the Writers Guild because the studio did not give them screenwriting credit. The Writers Guild awarded them "story by" credit, but the screenwriting credit remained with later writers. Generally, the studio gets final cut privileges as well.

No matter who you are or how you are attached to a project, once the film gets to the studio, you can be negotiated to a lower position or off the project altogether. The studio is the investor, and it calls the shots. If you are a new producer, the probability is high that studio executives will want their own producer on the project.

Those who want to understand more about the studio system should rent Christopher Guest's film *The Big Picture*, and read William Goldman's book *Adventures in the Screen Trade.* The studios are filled with major and minor executives in place between the corporate office and film production. There are executive vice presidents, senior vice presidents, and plain old vice presidents. Your picture can be green-lighted by one exec, then go into turnaround with his replacement. Getting decisions made is a hazardous journey, and the cliché, "No one gets in trouble by saying no," proves to be true more often than not.

MOTION PICTURE PRODUCTION AND THE INDEPENDENTS

What do we actually mean by the term "independent"? The traditional definition is a film that finds its production financing outside of the studios and free of studio creative control. The film may be distributed by a studio, but the filmmaker obtains the negative cost from other sources. This is the definition used in this book.

When three "Best Picture" Oscar nominations went to independent films in 1997 (four if you count Miramax's *The English Patient*), an odd change occurred via the media. Suddenly, they decided that the distributor was the definition. Not so. If Scott Hicks' producer Jane Scott spent several years raising $4.5 million for *Shine* from European and Australian sources, the film is independent. If Miramax acquires a film made with nonstudio financing, the film is independent.

A realignment of companies began in 1993 that has caused the structure of the industry to change at a faster pace than before. And a surge in relatively "mega" profits from low-budget films (production costs under $10 million) has encouraged the establishment of "independent" divisions at the studios. By acquiring or creating these divisions, the studios handle more films made by producers using financing from other sources. Disney, for example, purchased Miramax Films, maintaining it as an autonomous division. New Line Cinema (and its specialty division, Fine Line Pictures) and Castle Rock (director Rob Reiner's company) became part of Turner Broadcasting along with Turner Pictures. Universal and Polygram (80 percent owned by Philips N.V.) formed Gramercy Pictures to both distribute and finance "smaller" pictures. Gramercy's films, such as *Dead Man Walking*, were so successful that Polygram bought back Universal's share in 1995. Sony Pictures acquired Orion Classics, the only profitable segment of the original Orion Pictures, to form Sony Classics. Twentieth Century Fox formed Fox Searchlight and Fox Family Films. Metromedia, which owns Orion, bought The Samuel Goldwyn Company.

There is not room here to debate where DreamWorks SKG, formed in 1994 by Steven Spielberg, David Geffen, and Jeffrey Katzenberg, fits into these scenarios. The company, which aims to produce movies, music, new interactive entertainment, animated films, and television programs, has variously been called a studio, an independent and—my personal favorite—an independent studio. Capitalized at somewhere north of $2 billion, it is big. Yet, although it is in a class by itself, by our definition DreamWorks is still independent.

In 1996 Time Warner Corp. bought Turner Broadcasting. Originally, Time Warner reportedly planned to sell New Line for $1 billion (Turner paid $600 million for the company in 1993) to reduce the parent company's debt load. New Line's founder, Robert Shaye, and the other principals had always made their own production decisions, even as part of Turner Pictures. By the end of July 1997, New Line secured a $400 million loan through a consortium of foreign banks to provide self-sufficient production financing for New Line Cinema and Fine Line Features. The loan is non-recourse to Time-Warner, which means that the parent company has no repayment responsibility.

As part of an integrated company, specialty divisions have been able to give the studios the skill to acquire and distribute a different kind of film, while the studio is able to provide greater ancillary opportunities for the appropriate low-to-moderate budget films through their built-in distribution networks. The films remain independently funded, the prime definition of being an "independent." It is up to you, the reader, to track what has happened in the meantime.

How It Works

An independent film goes through the same production process as a studio film, from development to post-production. In this case, however, development and preproduction may involve only one or two people, and the entrepreneur, whether producer or director, maintains control over the final product. For the purposes of this discussion, we will assume that the entrepreneur at the helm of an independent film is the producer.

The independent producer is the manager of a small business enterprise. He or she must have business acumen for dealing with the investors, the actual money itself, and all the contracts involved during and after filming. The producer is totally responsible from inception to sale of the film and must have enough personal power to win the confidence of the director, talent, agents, attorneys, distributors, and anyone else involved in the film's business dealings. There are a myriad of things the producer must concentrate on every day. Funding sources require regular financial reports, and production problems crop up on a daily basis, even with the best-laid plans.

Traditionally, the fortunes of independent filmmakers have cycled up and down from year to year. For the past few years, they have been consistently up. In the late eighties, with the success of such films as *Dirty Dancing* (made for under $5 million, it earned more than $100 million worldwide) and *Look Who's Talking* (made for less than $10 million, it earned more than $200 million), the studios tried to distribute small films. With minimum releasing budgets of $5 million, however, they didn't have the experience or patience to let a small film find its market. Studios eventually lost interest in producing small films, and individual filmmakers and small independent companies took back their territory.

The Crying Game and *Four Weddings and a Funeral* began a new era for the independent filmmaker and distributor. The new strategy by the studios was (and is) to buy the successful independent distributors. As Miramax is spending Disney's money, their in-house productions become a gray area in terms of independent production. Many companies started with the success of a single film and its sequels. Carolco (which declared bankruptcy in 1996) built its reputation with the *Rambo* films, and New Line achieved prominence and clout with the *Nightmare on Elm Street* series. Other companies have been built on the partnership of a single director and a producer (or group of production executives) who consistently create high-quality, money-making films. Imagine Entertainment (Ron Howard and Brian Grazer) and Castle Rock Entertainment (Rob Reiner and his four partners) are prime examples. These companies have gone through too many changes since inception to track them all here—going public, establishing exclusive distribution deals with major studios, and sometimes even taking the studios in as investors. Imagine and Castle Rock have both taken steps to regain their creative and/or financial autonomy. The Imagine partners bought back stock and went private. Castle Rock, which had sold pieces of itself to several corporate entities, reached a merger agreement with Ted Turner in 1993, giving them more independence in the long run. Now the company, which is rumored to be incorporated into Time Warner, is looking for a white knight to free it.

Then there are the smaller independent producers, from the individual making a first film to small or medium-sized companies that produce multiple films each year. The smaller production companies usually raise money for one film at a time, although they may have many projects in different phases of development. Many independent companies are owned or controlled by the creative person, such as a writer–director or writer–producer, in combination with a financial partner or group. These independents make low-budget pictures, usually in the $25,000 to $5 million range. *Clerks* and *The Brothers McMullen* are at the lower end of the range, often called "no-budget."

Tracking the Independent Dollar

Before trying to look at the independent film industry as a separate segment, it is helpful to have a general view of how the money flows.

This information is probably the single most important factor that you will need to describe to potential investors. Wherever you insert this information in your plan, make sure that investors will understand the basic flow of dollars from the revenue sources to the producer.

Table 4.2 shows where the money comes from and where it goes. The figures given are for a fictional film and do not reflect the results of any specific film. This simplified example provides an overview of how this works. In this discussion, the distributor is at the top of the

Table 4.2 Tracking the Independent Dollar ($ millions)

Revenge of the Crazed Consultant*	
Domestic Box Office Gross	20.0
Exhibitor Share of Box Office (53%)	10.6
Distributor Share of Box Office (47%)	9.4
Revenue	
Domestic	
Theatrical Rentals (47% of Total Box Office)	9.4
Television	2.0
Video	3.5
Other (Planes, Schools, and so forth)	1.0
Foreign	
Theatrical	4.0
Television/video	5.5
Total Distributor Gross Revenue	25.4
Less:	
Budget	5.0
Prints and Advertising	8.3
Total Costs	13.3
Gross Income	12.1
Distributor's Fees	8.6
Net Producer/Investor Income before Taxes	3.5

*This is a fictional film.

"producer food chain," as all revenues come back to the distribution company first. The distributor's expenses (P&A) and fees (percentage of all revenue plus miscellaneous fees) come before the "total revenue to producer/investor" line, which is the "net profit."

The box office receipts for independent films are divided into exhibitor and distributor shares just as they are for studio films (see Table 4.1). Here, however, the split is 53/47 in favor of the exhibitor, rather than 50/50. This is an average figure for the total, although on a weekly basis the split may differ. Generally, independent companies do not have the same clout as the studios, and the exhibitor retains a greater portion of the receipts. In the example, of the $20 million in total U.S. box office, the distributor receives $9.4 million in rentals. This $9.4 million from the U.S. theatrical rentals represents only a portion of the total revenues flowing back to the distributor. Other revenues are added to this sum as they flow in (generally over a period of two years).

The film production costs and distribution fees are paid out as the money flows in. From the first revenues, the prints and ads (known as the first money out) are paid off. In this example, it is assumed that the prints and ads ("P&A") cost is covered by the distributor. Then, generally, the negative cost of the film is paid back to the investor. After the distributor has taken various fees, the producer and the investor divide the remaining money. Often the investor will live with a 90/10 or 80/20 split with the producer, while the initial investment is being paid off.

Pros and Cons

Independent filmmaking offers many advantages. The filmmaker has total control of the script and filming. Depending on agreements with distributors, it is usually the director's film to make and edit. Some filmmakers want to both direct and produce their movies; this is like working two 36-hour shifts within one 24-hour period. It is better to have a director direct and a producer produce, as this provides a system of checks and balances during production that approximates many of the pluses of the studio system. Nevertheless, the filmmaker is able to make these decisions for herself. And if she wants to distribute as well, preserving her cut and using her marketing plan, that is another option. Not necessarily a good one, as distribution is a specialty in itself, but still an option.

The disadvantages in independent filmmaking are the corollary opposites of the studio advantages. Because there is no cast of characters to fall back on for advice, the producer must have experience or must find someone who does. Either you will be the producer and run your production, or you will have to hire a producer. Before you hire anyone, you should understand how movies are made and how the financing works. Whether risking $50,000 or $5 million, an investor wants to feel that your company is capable of safeguarding his money. Someone must have the knowledge and the authority to make a final decision. Even if the money comes out of the producer's or the director's own pocket, it is advisable to have the required technical and business knowledge before starting.

Money is hard to find. Budgets must be calculated as precisely as possible in the beginning, because independent investors do not have the same deep pockets as the studios. The breakdown of the script determines the budget. When you present a budget to an investor, you promise that you will keep the movie within the budget, and the investor agrees only on the specified amount of money. The producer has an obligation to the investor to make sure that the movie does not run over budget.

PRODUCTION AND EXHIBITION FACTS AND FIGURES

The total gross box-office receipts for 1996 were $5.9 billion as reported by the MPAA. This figure represents admissions of 1.3 billion based on National Association of Theater Owners (NATO) average ticket prices. In the last five years, box office receipts have increased 23.1 percent, and the number of ticket buyers has increased 17.4 percent. These figures are available from the MPAA in Encino, CA.

Separating the gross dollars into studio and independent shares is another matter. The money always has been categorized by the classification of the distributor by studio or independent. Independent films, as we have said, are defined by their financing source, not their distributor. In order to estimate the total for independent films, you have to add those from all the independent distributors plus films that have been acquired by Miramax, Sony Classics, and distributing arms of the majors. As there is no database for "independent films acquired by studios," a precise figure is not possible. Calculating what we do know, however, the 1994 U.S. independent market is estimated at $843 million and the 1995 market at $1 billion. For 1996, AFMA (formerly called "The American Film Marketing Association") puts its annual estimate of total sales of independent films overseas at $1.7 billion.

Theatrical Exhibition

At the end of 1996, there were 29,960 theater screens (including drive-in screens) in the United States. This is an increase of approximately 22 percent since 1992, 40 percent since the mid-eighties, and more than 50 percent since the mid-seventies. Despite many ups and downs, such as the advent of television and the growth of the home video market, theatrical distribution has continued to prosper.

Film revenues from all other sources are driven by theatrical distribution. For pictures that skip the theatrical circuit and go directly into foreign markets or another medium, revenues are not likely to be as high as those for films with a history of U.S. box office revenues and promotion. The U.S. theatrical release of a film usually ends within the first year. Major studio films may be distributed to as many as 3,000 theaters in the first few weeks, but independent films start slower and build. The rentals will decline toward the end of a film's run, but they may very well increase during the first few months. It is not unusual for a smaller film to gain theaters as it becomes more popular.

Despite some common opinions, the exhibitor's basic desire is to see people sitting in the theater seats. There has been a lot of discussion about the strong-arm tactics that the major studios supposedly use to keep screens reserved for their use. (This is sometimes referred to as "block booking.") Exhibitors, however, have always maintained that they will show any film that they think their customers will pay to see. Depending on the location of the individual theater or the chain, local pressures or activities may play a part in the distributor's decision. Not all pictures are appropriate for all theaters.

Recent events have shown that independent films with good "buzz" (prerelease notices by reviewers and good public relations) and favorable word of mouth will not only survive but flourish. *The Crying Game* and *Strictly Ballroom* are prime examples. Both films started in a small number of theaters and cities. As audiences liked the films and told their friends about them, the movies were given wider release in chain theaters in more cities. Of course, good publicity gimmicks, such as *The Crying Game*'s "secret," do not hurt.

Future Trends

Table 4.3 shows estimates of future revenues as forecasted by Paul Kagan Associates Inc. at the end of June 1996. This projection, from *Motion Picture Investor* (PKBaseline, June 27, 1996) is based on the growth in these

Table 4.3 Estimated Distributor Revenue Streams ($ millions)

	Actual 1995	Projected 2001
Revenue Source		
Domestic		
Theatrical Rentals	2,660	3,479
Home Video	4,332	6,649
Broadcast Networks	286	380
Pay Television	1,135	1,920
Synidcated Television	350	310
Basic Cable	365	641
Foreign		
Theatrical Rentals	2,410	4,042
Home Video	3,760	5,802
Television Sales	2,140	3,706
Pay Television Sales	745	1,497
Other		
Cable/DBS/MMDS pay-per-view	124	1,417
Hotel/Airline/Other	46	70
Total Distributor Revenue	18,353	29,913

Source: Copyright© Paul Kagan Associates, Inc. Carmel, CA. Used with permission.

revenue sources from 1989 through 1995 and the first half of 1996. "It took seven years for the movie business to grow from $10 billion to $20 billion," the report asserts. "Our forecast calls for the industry to grow from $20 billion to $30 billion in about five years, with an annually compounded revenue growth rate between 1996 and 2001 of 8.6 percent."

As recently as 1987, according to the Kagan Group, more than 60 percent of movie distributor revenues came from the domestic markets. In 1995, the split between domestic and international revenue was almost 50/50. In the intervening years, the major exhibition chains set about multiplexing some of the countries in Europe and Australia. Other factors will influence demand over the next five years:

- Sales of digital video discs (DVDs) are projected to hit $3.4 billion by 2001 and possibly $6.8 billion worldwide.

- Direct broadcast satellite (DBS), already a force in Europe, is becoming a major delivery platform in the Asia/Pacific and Latin American markets, driving pay television and pay-per-view revenues.
- The United States has made controlling piracy of intellectual property (primarily videocassettes and music CDs sold in China) a top trade policy.

Using This Data

As there is a lapse of time from six months to a year, the known ancillary and foreign data will usually be two years behind by the time the book is published. The new technologies are volatile in their movements and can change in that time. DVDs, for example, came into the American market later than expected, because of the problems with determining standards. You can proceed to create your own projection for future trends based on whatever current data you have; such estimates often appear in the news media. However, keep in mind that whatever the model you develop for your business plan, you will have to explain the rationale behind it.

What impact will the new technologies have on theater attendance? Many different projections appear in the news media. CD-ROMs and a 500-channel universe seem less certain than they did four years ago. The Internet and Web-TV are currently the big items. Some experts argue that theater exhibition will always be the vehicle that drives the popularity of products played in the home and other outlets. Others say that theatrical exhibition will eventually be a thing of the past, although they do not give an exact date. Many are still waiting for that "killer application" that will have the same impact VHS did in the 1970s.

Theatrical exhibition is not likely to disappear during our lifetime, no matter what technological changes occur. What does this mean for you? Conventional wisdom used to say that films were recession-resistant. During wars and economic hard times, people went to the movies for some relief from the cares of the day. Movies were an inexpensive form of entertainment. Certainly, television and home video—both cheaper by far—have cut into this segment, but the numbers prove that seeing a film in the theater is still a favorite form of relaxation.

WHAT DO YOU TELL INVESTORS?

All business plans should include a general explanation of the industry and how it works. Whether you are planning $500,000 or $5-million movies, investors need to know how both the studio and the independent sectors work. Your business plan should also assure investors that this is a healthy industry. You will find conflicting opinions; it is your choice what information to use.

Whatever you tell the investor, be able to back it up with facts. As long as your rationale makes sense, your investor will feel secure that you know what you are talking about. That doesn't mean he or she will write the check, but at least he or she will trust you.

Tables and Graphs

A picture may be worth a thousand words, but 20 pictures are not necessarily worth 20,000. The introduction of user-friendly computer software has brought a new look to business plans. Unfortunately, many people have gone picture-crazy. They include tables and graphs where words might be better.

Graphs make up about three-fourths of one company's business plan. The graphs are very well done and to a certain extent do tell a story. The proposal, put together by an experienced consultant, is gorgeous and impressive—for what it is. But what is it? Imagine watching a silent film without the subtitles. You know what action is taking place, and you even have some vague idea of the story, but you don't know exactly who the characters are, what the plot is, or whether the resolution is a good one. Similarly, including a lot of graphs for the sake of making your proposal look nice has a point of diminishing returns.

There are certainly benefits to using tables and graphs, but there are no absolute rules about their use. Some of the rules for writing screenplays, however, do apply:

- Does this advance the plot?
- Is it gratuitous?
- Will the audience be able to follow it?

Ask yourself what relation your tables and graphs have to what investors need to know. For example, you could include a graph that shows the history of admissions per capita in the U.S. since 1950, but this might raise a red flag. Readers might suspect that you are trying to hide a lack of relevant research. You would only be fooling yourself. Investors looking for useful information will notice that it isn't there.

You will raise another red flag if you have multiple tables and graphs that are not accompanied by explanation. Graphic representations are not supposed to be self-explanatory; they are used to make the explanation more easily understood. There are two possible results: (1) The reader will be confused, or (2) the reader will think that you are confused. You might well be asked to explain your data. Won't that be exciting?

5

The Markets and Marketing

But the Devil whoops, as he whooped of old: It's clever but is it art?

RUDYARD KIPLING

You can take the 5 billion people in the world as a potential movie-going population, but very few filmmakers have expected to sell tickets to all of them—that is, until *Jurassic Park* pushed the box office frontier farther than ever before in 1993. It earned more than $750 million worldwide. You didn't need English or have to know anything about history to enjoy this film. It had something for everyone who was old enough to watch it. Then, in 1996, *Independence Day* racked up $726 million worldwide.

What does this mean to you, the independent? Not much, except that studios are concentrating on the very high budget end. *Titanic*, yet to be released as this book is being written, will reportedly set a new record at $200 million (that's negative cost, not grosses). This emphasis leaves a much larger part of the theatrical ballpark for the independent filmmaker making low- to medium-budget movies. And the home runs being hit in the past year have opened the game to many more players. Recently Steven Spielberg told *Premiere Magazine*,

> *It's getting to the point where only two kinds of movies are being made—the tentpole summer or Christmas movies or the sequels, and the audacious little Gramercy, Fine Line or Miramax films. It's like there's an upper class, a poverty class and no middle class. We are squeezing out the Hollywood middle class, allowing only the $70m plus films or the $10m minus films.*

In the past three years, more films financed by foreign companies and consortiums of investors have been $30 million plus films. Realistically, though, your potential of having Keanu Reeves star in your adventure film is low. In fact, if you are a neophyte, it is probably suicide. In this chapter, it is assumed that you are making a film for less than $10 million, and that your film is not made for a mass audience, but rather fits into a narrower genre category.

This chapter looks at your market and your marketing. Do not confuse these two concepts. The *market* for your film comprises those people who are going to buy tickets. We will be looking at the potential popularity of whatever themes and styles your films represent. On the other hand, *marketing* involves selling your idea to the people who can help you get the film made. (To make these terms more confusing, this book also refers to the *markets*—that is, where you go to sell your film.)

In the last section of your business plan, you defined the industry as a whole and independent film as a segment of it. Now you will build on that definition by further dividing your industry segment. Your segment may not be as global in size as "everyone," but it has its own value. You will also take the products that you described in an earlier section and use their components to pinpoint your market. This analysis gives you a base for later estimating those very important ticket sales.

MARKET SEGMENT

Your market segment, or niche, is that part of the total moviegoing population that you expect to see the film. You need to identify, for yourself and those reading your proposal, the size and population characteristics of this segment. By devising a snapshot of your film's likely audience, you will be able to determine its ability, first, to survive and, second, to succeed. Who are the end users of your film—that is, the ticket buyers—and how many of them are there likely to be? Before you worry about marketing strategies and distribution channels, create a picture of the potential size of your market's population. How can you do this? Very carefully. But do not worry. It is easier than you think; it just takes work. You do not need to have inside information or to live in Los Angeles to do this. Research is your tool.

Having divided the industry into parts, you now need to divide your segment into smaller pieces. In looking at this piece of the market, ask yourself these questions:

- How large a population segment is likely to see my film?
- What size budget is reasonable vis-à-vis the size of this segment?

Defining Your Segment

Filmmakers would like to appeal to everyone, and some mainstream films reach that goal. It is said that it is the big-budget action/adventure films that create the highest box office grosses. This is true to a certain extent; the more money you spend, the bigger the audience you will attract—and the bigger the audience you will *need* to attract. An independent film, for the most part, will attract moviegoers from one or two identifiable segments of the audience. To understand how to focus your marketing efforts, you will have to do a little research. You do not have to be a research expert, but a little light investigation will help make you and your investor wiser and wealthier.

Creating a profile of your target market in terms of audience might include the following:

- Popular film genres
- Age
- Sex
- Personal preferences
- Successful budget parameters

To Pigeonhole or Not to Pigeonhole

Your identification of the target audience for your film begins when you select the genre of the film. The term "genre" refers to films that can be clustered together because of a specific similarity. For example, *Westerns* are generally movies that take place in a specific time period and have a similar style. Today, *alternative-lifestyle films* have gay and lesbian themes; in a different generation, the term might have been used for films about flower children. The genre name offers the advantage of giving your film a potential audience pool.

Many writers and directors believe that categorizing their films is not only meaningless but in some cases demeaning. There are always filmmakers who say, "My picture is different and can't be compared to any other films." This attitude is reminiscent of the entrepreneurs who say they have no competition. All films can be compared, and you do have competition.

Genres can be big or small. Action/adventure is considered the most popular genre. Family films run a close second. These were once referred to as children's films; today, the term "family" reflects a wider scope of age range and interests. Comedies cross many lines, and these movies often carry descriptive adjectives, such as "family," "romantic," or "black," to further narrow the category. Defining the genre of a particular film can become unnecessarily complicated. In trying to be precise about identifying a film, the filmmaker may call it a romance/comedy/adventure. This description is guaranteed to leave out no one. It covers all the bases. What film does this describe? Answer: *Romancing the Stone*.

How do you classify those filmmakers who have a specific style all their own? Often, such a filmmaker becomes a genre. Saying a movie will be a Woody Allen film, a Robert Altman film, a John Waters film, or a Merchant–Ivory film creates a frame of reference for the particular experience moviegoers will have. These days, you can even have a producer genre. For example, a Joel Silver film would immediately be envisioned as another *Die Hard* or *Lethal Weapon*. This does not mean that the film will not fit into a customary genre, such as comedy or relationship films. However, the filmmaker is so identified with a style of experience that the audience will pick the film for the director rather than anything else. If you feel that your style is akin to a particular director's niche, you can draw from that audience.

Why bother identifying the genre for your film? These frames of reference not only indicate the type of theatrical experience moviegoers will have, they also help you explain where your film falls in the distribution and finance model. One of the challenges you face with your business plan is being understood. You must be certain that you convey your meaning correctly to investors. It is important, therefore, that you define your terms so that everyone is talking about the same thing.

Art versus Specialty

I recently participated in a discussion on whether independent films are by definition "art" films and, if they are, what an art film is. One person claimed that Federico Fellini and art films were one and the same. Someone else said that they "explain human foibles in an intellectual way." These pages do not contain a definitive definition for the word "art," but it is an important term to examine further.

In recent times, production and distribution companies have preferred the term "specialty" for their films rather than "art-house"—and with good reason. "Art" may bring to mind a very narrow vision of a type of film. Many would assume the film to be a boring, bogged-down film for the intellectually intense. "Specialty," on the other hand, is a broader term without these negative connotations. Until you define it, there may be no frame of reference for the investor. Creating a definitive description that everyone agrees with would be impossible. In writing your business plan, you have to find whatever phrases and film references that best convey your meaning.

I have been involved with proposals for companies that intended to be like The Samuel Goldwyn Company (before it was acquired by Metromedia) or Fine Line Pictures (before it was acquired by Time Warner). What did we start with? We used those companies to define the genre. For example, you could write the following as your introduction:

> *We define the specialty market by the types of films acquired by October Films and Sony Classics. Our films have a sensitivity of story and a delicate balance of characters that require unique handling. Therefore, our audience will be the same people who saw* Secrets and Lies, The Spitfire Grill, The Last Seduction *and* Persuasion.

These pictures may have nothing in common in story or overall theme, but they are used to present a backdrop for the discussion; they give readers something to relate to. Of course, October and Sony Classics do not have a lock on specialty films. Which companies you use for comparison depends on your feeling about their products and on the films that you want to use for comparison.

An important aspect of specialty films is their distribution (and, consequently, revenue) potential. In recent years, the scope of specialty films has widened tremendously. For example, in a review of Jane Campion's film *The Piano*, a critic referred to it as the "art-house hit of the year." (As noted earlier, "specialty" is probably a better term to use; "art-house" may send the wrong message about the box office potential of the film.) Typically, there are one or two "art houses" in a town—usually small theaters with up to 200 seats. When *The Piano* was awarded the Palme d'Or at Cannes and received an Academy Award nomination for best picture in the United States (the movie eventually won three Oscars), its distributor, Miramax, did not allow it to languish in a few small theaters. It played on over 500 screens in all types of venues across the country.

Genre History

When describing the history of a particular genre, you need not go back to Tom Mix (ask your grandmother). For the most part, your primary reference period should be the last two to three years. Some genres, such as action/adventure or comedy, are always going strong. They are always popular in one form or another. This is not the case with other genres, however.

Take Westerns, for example. This genre, once popular, had been languishing until recently. The general wisdom was that Westerns did not make money. Before the success of Kevin Costner and Jim Wilson with *Dances with Wolves,* therefore, it was hard to get the investment community interested in the genre. The last major Western had been *Silverado* in 1985. Although the film received favorable critical reviews, it was not considered a financial success.

Timing is everything. Now money is available everywhere, not only for the traditional "cowboy-loves-his-horse" movie, but for Westerns with all-female casts as well. Filmmakers who had been trying to get Western-style films made for four or five years suddenly found interested investors. Unfortunately, they also found a lot more competition than existed previously.

Suppose you wanted to make a Western before *Dances with Wolves* was released. How would you have convinced someone that your film would be successful? There are several techniques you could use.

1. *Emphasize other elements:* "Boy Goes West is a coming-of-age film set in the modern Southwest." In this case, you would discuss the film in terms of the coming-of-age genre, which has been popular in recent years. You could use a list of similar films for comparison.
2. *Redefine the genre:* "Girl Goes West is the saga of a young woman who goes to the contemporary Southwest." Here, you would make an end run around the issue of the Old West not being a popular theme. In addition, you could emphasize the

subplot, focusing on your heroine finding herself, seeking love, or looking for vampires.

3. *Override the Western locale:* "*Murder at the Canteen* is a mystery or suspense thriller set in Texas." If the setting has little to do with the storyline, it need not be part of your market description. You can compare your film to other murder or suspense thrillers, whatever their setting. These genres are forever popular and do not tend to have cycles.

4. *Use the cycle theory:* "*West Is West* is a Western of the old school. Despite the absence of Westerns in recent years, we believe this film can bring the genre back." Here you are attacking the main problem head on (lack of financially successful Westerns) rather than hoping that the reader isn't sophisticated enough to know.

More about Cycles

The last technique is not a spurious argument. The popularity of particular genres rises and falls in cycles. For example, horror films, which made up 24 percent of the product at the 1989 American Film Market, were less than 3 percent of the total in 1993. (Interestingly, the genre fell out of favor in the book industry at the same time.) Statistics like these, by the way, can be part of your extended discussion.

A successful film often inspires a number of similar films that try to capitalize on the popularity of the original. *Jagged Edge*, for example, was released in 1985. It grossed $40 million in the United States and encouraged the proliferation of a series of suspense films over the next three years, including *Fatal Attraction*. Considering the length of time from development to release, the market may be glutted with a particular type of film for two or three years. When this happens, the audience may reach a saturation point and simply stop going to see films of that genre. Then someone comes along with a well-crafted film that makes money, and the cycle begins again.

Who Is Going to See This Film?

Do you know the age and sex of the person most likely to see your film? Market research properly belongs in the hands of the person doing the actual marketing (probably the distributor), but you can estimate the appeal of your potential market based on its age groups. For example, one animated film may be aimed primarily at children

10 and under. Another animated film, with a slightly more hip theme and a pop music soundtrack, may entertain children but also draw in teenagers and young adults. *FernGully,* with its environmental theme, hoped to capture the politically green adult audience. Disney's hit *Beauty and the Beast* was geared for and received the entire age population, from the very young to the very old. Ralph Bakshi's *Fritz the Cat* was geared to an audience all its own.

Coming-of-age films are targeted toward an affluent and sizable group—teenagers. The same audience is also responsible for the popularity of action/adventure films, the *Police Academy* series, comic fantasies such as *Bill & Ted's Excellent Adventure,* and many other high-grossing films. Teenage movies are traditionally released at the beginning of the summer when schools are out and kids have a lot of time to go to the theater.

From the early seventies to the mid-eighties, the philosophy of studios was to make films for the teen and young adult market—usually defined as people between the ages of 12 and 24. Then the average age of audiences started to change. In the mid-eighties, teenagers who had once commanded up to 32 percent of the market fell to 25 percent. The studios began to recognize adult moviegoers as a sizable population. Island Film's *Mona Lisa,* a British import, was one of the first films to signal the change in the mid-eighties.

Various independent distributors began to forge their growth on films with adult themes (not to be confused with porn). Merchant–Ivory's *Howards End,* a 1992 release based on a 1910 E.M. Forster novel, scored $26 million in grosses against a budget of $7.75 million. Emma Thompson gave the picture more status when she won the Academy Award for Best Actress. In fact, the general success of Merchant–Ivory films over the past 30 years is one more indication of the market for quality films. And in the past five years, everything that Jane Austen ever wrote has been made into theatrical feature films and cable miniseries.

Special Niche Groups

Certain groups of films initially appeal to a small segment of the population and grow to become crossover, mainstream films. The high cost structures of the studios inhibit their ability to exploit smaller, underdeveloped markets, but independent filmmakers have the ability to take chances. They can make a low-budget or even a "nonbudget" film to play to a tiny initial market. If the film and its theme catch on, the audience grows, and the film genre crosses over to a larger portion of the public. Subsequent films of that type draw on the larger audience.

One such niche has been black-themed films. Until Spike Lee's *She's Gotta Have It* in 1986, production companies and distributors did not consider there to be a significant market for black-themed films. The Lee film, which was made for $175,000 and grossed $7 million in the United States, was the starting point for a genre that has been growing ever since.

Next came Robert Townsend's *Hollywood Shuffle* in 1987. The story of Robert Townsend using his credit cards (to the tune of $40,000) along with personal savings to finance the movie has become part of independent film folklore. It is told in great detail in David Rosen's book, *Off Hollywood*. Townsend says that with one month left before his credit card bills came due, he rented the Writers Guild screening room and invited everyone in the industry, including the secretaries and gofers who actually started the "buzz." The Samuel Goldwyn Company signed on as distributor, and the rest is history. The film gained a box office of $7 million, compared to a negative cost of around $100,000, similar to the results of *She's Gotta Have It.*

Production companies and distributors began not only to court these directors but also to look for other black filmmakers. Money became available for bigger budgets, and the films moved into the mainstream. One of the interesting and frustrating things about niche markets is that the audience may already be there, but no one is willing to test the waters.

A business plan written in 1990 by an investment banking firm seeking to start a company capitalized on this new market with the following well-crafted explanation:

> *These films consistently draw both their target audience and the general audience. . . . The demand for niche films targeted toward this segment far outpaces the supply of these films. This genre is moving out of its infancy, however, as major studios realize its potential profitability. Black filmmakers and other black talent are moving out of the shadows of Hollywood and are gaining increasing respect and recognition for their creative talents.*

Notice that the writer has managed to combine facts with interesting writing. You can always incorporate a few lyrical phrases in a business proposal, as long as you do not get carried away with it.

Another niche that has come to the fore recently is alternative-lifestyle films. For years, films with gay or lesbian themes were relegated to small theaters in neighborhoods with largely homosexual populations and were more or less shunned by traditional distribution outlets. As social attitudes began to change, however, public interest in AIDS convinced television executives to present the theme in more MOWs. It was a short step from there to features aimed at a more mainstream audience being produced and self-distributed by producers.

In 1987 and 1988, several films with homosexual scenes or major characters were popular. The 1988 film *Torch Song Trilogy*, which had been a success on the theatrical stage, found acceptance as a New Line release. In 1990, *Longtime Companion*, a drama financed by American Playhouse, was an award winner at the Sundance Film Festival and an Oscar nominee. Next was 1991's *My Own Private Idaho*, a successful feature with significant gay content. In 1992, *Fried Green Tomatoes*, one of the first mainstream films with a lesbian theme, did exceptionally well both critically and financially. An earlier film, *Desert Hearts*, with more explicit lesbian material, had done well critically but not commercially. *Fried Green Tomatoes* was based on a book whose explicit scenes were toned down for the film. Nevertheless, it signaled that the alternative-lifestyle genre would not keep people out of the theaters.

A business plan written in early 1992 by a company that intended to make lesbian-themed films used the success of *Fried Green Tomatoes* as a selling point:

> We believe that with the current interest in gay/lesbian issues as well as women's issues, films with lesbian themes will be able to cross over into mainstream acceptance and profitability. A recent film with an implied lesbian relationship between its two lead characters, Fried Green Tomatoes, with an approximate budget of $12 million, has rentals to date of $35.3 million from theatrical distribution in the first four months of release. . . . We plan to begin with a $500,000 film that will benefit from exposure at the festivals. With distribution in limited runs in "specialty" theaters throughout the United States, sales of videocassettes by gay/lesbian distribution companies and the several hundred gay and lesbian bookstores throughout the United States and Canada will increase total revenues for the film.

Here the producers have managed to hedge their bets. When this plan was written, some of the recent profitable low-budget films with frank lesbian themes, such as *Claire of the Moon*, had not yet been released. The company's rationale was that the market appeared to be there. In lieu of definite proof, however, the producers offered statistics on the gay/lesbian population to show that a well-made movie with a small budget ($500,000) could count on breaking even at the very least.

Production Cost

When writing a business plan, you need to find as many ways to support your argument as possible. A valid comparison for films is the amount of the production (negative) cost. In some cases, the cost is additional confirmation for your assertions; in other instances, it may be your only argument. There are as many configurations of a film's budget as there are producers. No two situations are ever alike. So we will take the most common cases and let you extrapolate from there.

Case 1: Similar Films, Similar Budgets

Suppose you are proposing to make black-themed films after Spike Lee, Robert Townsend, and the Hudlin brothers exploded on the scene but before John Singleton, Jackson-McHenry, and others appeared. At that time, you would be looking at the films listed in Table 5.1.

As long as your films will stay within the same budget range, under $6 million, you have a direct comparison. Your films should be able to make the same or better revenues. When preparing your proposal, the first step is to read every interview with the filmmakers that you can find. You will usually be able to find information on how they made their pictures work—creating a production budget, finding a distributor, and getting by on a low budget. This information will help you verbalize your strategy. You might say something like the following:

> *The acceptance of Spike Lee by the studios shows that black-themed films have a mainstream audience. Yet there is a small number of African-American film-*

Table 5.1 Selected Black-Themed Films as of 1990 ($ millions)

Film	Year	Distributor	U.S. Box Office Gross	Negative Cost
She's Gotta Have It	1986	Island	7.3	0.2
Hollywood Shuffle	1987	Goldwyn	5.2	0.1
School Daze	1988	Columbia	7.1	5.6
I'm Gonna Git You Sucka	1988	MGM/UA	10.7	4.3
Do the Right Thing	1988	Universal	26.5	6.0
House Party	1990	New Line	26.4	2.6

Note: These are the films used in the business plan quoted above.

makers in the arena at this time. The market is open for more producers and directors to take up that slack. Considering the number of African-Americans in the total population, films with budgets of less than $6 million have less risk on the downside. The potential for having a breakout film gets higher with the release of each successful film.

Case 2: Similar Films, Higher Budgets

If your film has a story or theme similar to that of others but will be made with a significantly higher budget, you will have to attach more elements to it. If you have a well-known director or actors who will draw some attention, be sure to mention them. For a film with a budget of up to $1 or $2 million, both the director and the stars can be unknown; the film will rely totally on its story and quality. For a larger film, though, story and quality still matter, but box office names become more important. The director may be one of these names—"another Arthur Artiste picture." In this case, you might say something like the following:

> *The movies of Spike Lee and Robert Townsend show that there is a significant market for films with black heroes and heroines. We plan to exploit this market by using the name recognition of our director, Arthur Artiste. With Handsome Devil and Linda Lovely as the leads in our first film, the company will be able to establish itself immediately as a leading producer of quality films.*

Case 3: Different Films, Moderate Budgets

There may be a ceiling on the ability of niche films to grab the market. One strategy in this case is to start with moderate budgets that have mainstream potential. For this example, we will assume that you will start with a $5-million movie and move up to a much broader market. Always keep your genre in mind in addition to all the factors mentioned in Case 2. You might try something like the following:

> *It has become clear in the past five years that the market for black-themed films is growing. We intend to create movies that cross over into a larger, more mainstream market segment. Our films, romantic comedies, will reach an even broader population of moviegoers than previous black-themed films.*

These case examples focused on one particular niche to give you a better idea of how these explanations vary. There are as many variations as there are fish in the sea. The point is that you should build on what exists. No matter what your niche market—and it may be a specialized one that has not really been explored yet—the same principles apply. Take the experience of similar films and use it to your advantage.

Even with these three cases, a discussion of the success of similarly budgeted films is in order. For example, in the business plan mentioned earlier for gay/lesbian films, the producers planned to make three films over a five-year period with a budget of $500,000 for the first film, $2 million for the second, and $7 million for the third. Their argument was that the company would gain a reputation from the first film and would use that to grow on as the subject matter became part of a continually expanding market. Because there were no gay/lesbian films made with $7-million budgets to use for comparison, they created tables of other niche films with similar budgets.

Detailed tables showing the actual results of other films with similar budgets appropriately belong in the financial section of your plan. Here, however, you can use the summary information to build a story. Gather in comparative market information to prove the size and extent of the audience for your film. What if you do not know the budgets of the films you are going to make? Your case will be much weaker, but you can still develop a rationale. Showing the results of films at various budgets will help. The other elements of your company, as described in Chapter 3, can bring more credence to your proposal. If you have well-known directors or actors committed to your projects, you can use their previous films to describe a segment of the market.

MARKETING STRATEGY

Marketing strategy is usually defined as the techniques used to make the end user aware of a product. In film, you have more than one potential end user—more than one person who might queue up to the box office to buy a ticket. If you cannot reach these people, though, they will not be in that line. To give them that opportunity, you use your business plan to reach an intermediate end user—the money. The ticket buyer will not read your business plan. Instead, your marketing is aimed at entities that might provide the money to make those ticket purchases possible. First, we'll look at your own strategies for getting the film made. Then, we'll look at some of the marketing tactics that distributors and producers may use for the film.

Experts often talk about the four Ps of marketing: product, price, place, and promotion. We have already touched on the first three in this section. In the marketing section of your business plan, you also want to focus on promotion. Eventually, the distributor probably will be responsible for the specific tactics of fulfilling a marketing plan, but you can describe for investors what some of these tactics might be.

Market Research

As cognizant as investors or distributors might be about the emergence of a niche market, they may not know its true scope. Part of the promotion of your company is to obtain as much market research data as possible to bolster your contentions. In the normal course of finding financing for one film, this activity is helpful but not necessary. In putting together a company, however, you have different obligations and responsibilities. Gathering data on the feasibility of your concept is one of them. Part of that information is contained in your description of the market segment. However, you can go a step farther and get real facts and figures.

There are many formal and informal ways to gather information. Many of them are right in your own backyard. You can gain a lot of knowledge with a minimum of time and effort if you know how. Granted, some of these tricks of the trade are easier the closer you are to Hollywood or New York, but with the proliferation of events to which "Hollywoodites" travel, being from another city is not a good excuse for failing to do adequate research. Your task may be a little harder, but you can still accomplish it.

Reading—A Lost Art

The hardest idea to get across to many filmmakers is that they need to become prolific readers. Many creative folks are too busy doing their own thing to take time out to read. This is a big mistake. There is a lot of information available to you if you will take the time and trouble to find it. Even seasoned professionals say, "But I don't have time." The truth is that you cannot afford not to have time.

The primary source for people in the film business is the trade papers, primarily *The Hollywood Reporter* and *Daily Variety*. Those who are serious about having a business or even participating in the industry will do themselves a favor by subscribing to both papers. Many people argue, "I can't afford it," but in the long run, it will be the cheapest way for you to get the most information.

The trades have the news articles that tell you who is doing what with whom and how much it is going to cost. If you follow these sources carefully, you can pull out enough data to fill in the basic financials for any package. Nestled among the press releases and gossip are real facts on the production costs of many films and descriptions of how the producers found their financing. The reviews of new movies often make comparisons to similar films or discuss breakthrough pictures in terms of their genres. Recent examples are the low-budget films *Sling Blade* ($1.35 million) and *Shine* ($4 million). The films generated much comment in the media on the acceptability of making films about the mentally deficient and/or disturbed. On another front, a film that seemed universally accepted was *The Adventures of Priscilla, Queen of the Desert*, the story about two drag queens and a transsexual taking their act on the road in Australia. If you had a film about drag queens ready to go (I happen to know someone who did), this was the time to find an investor.

Both of the trade papers publish lists of films in production, preproduction, and development. From the production columns, you can learn what genres of films are being made and with what types of casts. Some of the preproduction material is real and some is fantasy, but it gives you a fair idea of what people want to produce. You can list your films in the development columns free of charge. Many filmmakers have gotten contacts with production companies and distributors that way. Placing announcements also gives private investors a chance to hear about you. Many people with the ability to finance films choose to remain incognito; otherwise, they would be deluged with unwanted phone calls or scripts. They do read the trades, however, and it gives them the opportunity to contact producers whose stories interest them. Admittedly, this may be a long shot, but it does not cost you anything, and it gets your name out there.

One interesting quirk about Hollywood—and this is probably true of other places as well—is that people have more respect for names they recognize than for those that are unfamiliar. They will not necessarily remember where they saw or heard your name, but familiarity results in returned phone calls. Therefore, any opportunity to get your name in print is helpful.

Another benefit of reading the trades is that you learn who the movers and shakers are. Take the case of Robert Rodriguez, writer–director of the $7,000 miracle film, *El Mariachi*. He did not know any agents or others in Los Angeles, but he saw the name of Robert Newman, an agent at ICM (one of the two largest talent agencies in the entertainment business), in the trade papers and sent him the film as a sample director's reel. Newman took it to Columbia.

Besides the industry publications, you can find a lot of information in regular monthly magazines that have no direct connection to the film industry. Let's look at just a small sampling of magazines: Interviews with producers or directors of independent films and articles with business statistics were published recently in such non-entertainment publications as *New York Magazine, Vanity Fair, Time, Newsweek,* and *Forbes.* Local daily newspapers and *USA Today,* a national daily, also carry interviews in their entertainment and business sections. The proliferation of publications on the Internet has made this information far more accessible and, in many cases, free. Be alert; wherever you are, there is information available.

Networking

My first Sundance Film Festival was also my first entertainment industry event. Until then, I had worked in "real business," creating business plans and corporate strategies. Although I will admit to mixing and mingling at meetings before, I had never tried to "work a town." I knew no one, and had a general feeling of nausea as I got off the plane. On the shuttle to Park City, everyone was silent. Finally, I asked a gentleman sitting behind me if it was his first trip. He and his friend turned out to be film commissioners. We chatted the rest of the way. That night I went with them to the opening night gathering and met more people. The next day, I chatted with those people and learned a lot about how they had financed their films and other salient information. Had I not spoken to the first two people, I might never have met the rest. The concept of networking this way can be very scary, but you can do it. Being friendly is not only a way to gather information, but also to make yourself known to others.

Why do you want to network? Your best sources of information may be going to seminars, luncheons, industry meetings, festivals, and markets. Besides listening to whatever public speaking occurs, you should go up and introduce yourself to the speakers, and you should mix with other people in the room.

There is no better source for information than other independent filmmakers. Whenever you have a chance to meet filmmakers, grill them for advice and facts. People like to talk about their experiences and, especially, their successes. (If this were not the case, I would not be able to get well-known filmmakers for my classes and seminars.) You will learn more from someone who has done what you are interested in than from all the books in the world.

Libraries and Computer Sources

Like reading, another lost art appears to be the ability to do research in a library. I was stunned to find out that graduate students have never heard of the *Business Periodicals Index* and other common library reference books.

In writing a business plan, you must be concerned with more than just film grosses. You must be able to discuss the markets, the environment, ethnic groups, population figures, societal trends—whatever is pertinent to your projects and to your ticket buyers. In addition, a business plan should contain specifics about other companies, industry mergers and acquisitions, new industries, and so on.

The first sources for this information are all those articles and books you never read or even knew existed. Besides visiting bookstores, go to your local library, a film-school library, or a general university library. If you live near Los Angeles, you have the added advantage of the library of the Academy of Motion Picture Arts and Sciences. Look up your subject in the *Business Periodicals Index* and other periodical guides in the library. Many libraries have systems that allow you to do a computerized search of subjects. Finally, do not forget your friendly librarians; they are there to help you.

If you are an upwardly mobile technoid, you can make use of computer programs, such as CD-ROMs that will let you search for movie information by title and subject. Through your computer, you can patch into the Internet and use online services to do library searches without ever leaving home. Computerized searches of this type are more expensive than those you do yourself at the library, since they require you to own equipment and purchase online services. But you can continue writing your business plan while an electronic brain does your research. Companies reached through the Internet, such as Baseline, allow you to download box office grosses and other data.

Promoting Yourself and Your Project

We make our own opportunities, as every overnight success will tell you. By doing all that market research, you have prepared yourself for two things:

- Quantifying your market segment
- Approaching others with your project

At the beginning of this chapter, we talked about the market segment; now it is time to focus on marketing yourself and your project. As noted before, your goal is to find the money or links to the money.

Arm Yourself with Ammunition

As a good promoter, there are certain materials you can prepare before seeking out contacts. Business cards, sell sheets, press kits, and director's reels are among the promotional materials you might use. Some film-makers have even made a 45-minute version of the film itself, often on videotape, for promotion. For first-time filmmakers with no other footage to show, putting a long treatment on film may be the way to go.

More Networking

The materials just described serve to get you into in-depth meetings. Whether your aim is to sell a single film or to create interest in your company's group of films, the first step is to evoke interest. Making contacts is your objective—wherever you are. Earlier we talked about networking as a means of gathering information. Another purpose is to unearth those money sources—wherever they are.

People with like interests tend to congregate in the same places; therefore, entertainment-related gatherings are your most likely place for success. Although potential investors are not likely to be in atten-dance, their friends and acquaintances probably are. Festivals and markets are critical for whatever you are selling, and working them is of the utmost importance. You do not want to be carrying around business plans, handing them to everyone who says, "I can get you a deal." That is why you bother with the materials described earlier. Those are the items you hand to people you meet.

Common sense will stand you in good stead in attending markets and festivals. There is no trick to meeting and greeting, no secret handshakes or passwords. When you attend a market, remember that a distributor's goal in being there is not to meet you; it is to sell product. Here are guidelines for you to follow:

- *Be prepared:* Bring your short-term promotional materials, and bone up on who is who before you go. Let your fingers do some walking through the trades.
- *Be aware:* Distribution companies usually focus on certain types of films. Look at their posters and at the items listed in

their market catalogs. Try to match your films to their inventory. After all, the distributor is your shortest route to those foreign buyers and presales.

- *Be inquisitive:* Ask questions of everyone you meet—in an office, in the lobby, on the street. Try to discover the person's qualifications before spilling your guts about your plans and projects, however.
- *Be considerate:* In introducing yourself to distributors, pick slack times. Very early in the day and at the end of the day are best. Whenever you reach a distributor's display room, notice if buyers are there. If they are, go back later.
- *Be succinct:* Keep discussion short and sweet. Your objective is to get a meeting at a later time. You want your prey to feel relaxed and be attentive. Try for a meeting at the distributor's office.
- *Be dubious:* Lots of people are milling around towns and lobbies pretending to be something they are not. It may be a big rush for some people to say that they have a million dollars to invest and watch you get all excited. Listen carefully. Take cards and try to verify the facts afterward. Do not give your scripts or proposals to anyone unless you can validate their credentials.

6

Distribution

It is well known what a middleman is: he is the man who bamboozles one party and plunders the other.

BENJAMIN DISRAELI
Speech at Maynooth, England, April 11, 1845

Long before Carl Laemmle produced his first maverick film, middlemen existed (as did agents, attorneys, and litigation). These intermediaries bought low and sold high even then. Among the most maligned of all entrepreneurs, middlemen are still harshly criticized for doing their job.

· Motion picture distributors are middlemen, and they are a curious lot. They are viewed either as people of tremendous skill nourishing the growth of business or as flimflam artists reaping obscene profits. Like politicians, distributors are sometimes seen as a necessary evil. They perform an important function, however, without which many businesses, and certainly filmmakers, would not thrive.

When writing your business plan, you will need to explain the distribution system. As with other elements of the plan, you should proceed on the assumption that your reader does not know how the system works. Wrong assumptions on either side could block the progress of your films and your company.

This chapter looks at distribution strategies in general, glances briefly at studio distribution, and examines independent distribution in some depth.

WHAT IS A DISTRIBUTOR?

History does not tell us when the term "distributor" began to be used. If you look through any other business plan book, chances are you will not see a category for distribution. Examine the table of contents and browse through the index; distributors are not there. All industries have wholesalers, but their role is more narrowly defined than in the film world. Elsewhere, wholesalers are customers for the manufacturer. They buy inventory product at discount prices, add a price markup, and resell at the higher price. In this sense, these intermediaries are considered just another one of the channels for getting the product to market. They are not involved in making artistic decisions about the product, changing the name for better marketing, or obtaining premanufacturing financing.

The significant purpose of middlemen, notes Philip Kotler, a marketing expert, "boils down to their superior efficiency in the basic marketing tasks and functions. [They] offer the producer more than he can usually achieve on his own."[1] All of this is true of film distributors, but they are also much more. Film distributors have tremendous power, and in independent film, their impact is magnified. Studios normally have committees and different levels of people making a decision. In an independent distribution company, one person, with no one to answer to, may determine the entire course of your film. The distributor has the ability to influence script changes, casting decisions, final edits, and marketing strategies; in addition, distributors often are intimately involved in the financing of the film.

Before the audience can buy a ticket or rent a video, the movie has to get off the producer's desk and into the movie theaters. This method of circulation is called distribution. Simply put, it is the business of selling the film to various media, such as theatrical, cable, video, pay-per-view, television, nontheatrical (army bases, airplanes, ships at sea, and so on), and, soon, CDs. But it is not simply done. The distributor must be a salesperson, an entrepreneur, a skillful negotiator and a raconteur, and must have a sixth sense about matching the buyer with the product.

Film Rights: The "rights" of a film stem from the ownership of the copyright, which endows the legal use of the film on the copyright holder. Having secured a formal copyright, the producer contractually licenses, or rents, the film to a distributor for a specific length of time. The producer can relinquish all control of the film by shifting the

---

[1]Philip Kotler, *Marketing Management* (p. 279). Englewood Cliffs, NJ: Prentice-Hall, 1976.

entire copyright to the distributor in perpetuity, or he or she can license a specific right, such as domestic, foreign, video, cable, television, satellite, or telephone (it's coming), to the distributor for a specific length of time. In return, the distributor collects the rental monies or ancillary fees and remits the producer's share.

Armed with whatever film rights they have acquired, distributors go about the business of relicensing the film to the various media. The U.S. theatrical box office is the backbone in the chain of revenues for any film. All ancillary results are driven by the domestic theatrical release. Some products are made to skip that step and go directly to video or foreign markets, but the value of a film in any other media and territories is generally greater with a good theatrical release. Even a small theatrical release can increase the value to buyers of an otherwise unknown film.

STUDIO DISTRIBUTION

How It Works

The major studios (and the larger production companies) each have their own distribution divisions. They not only release their own films, but occasionally acquire other films as well. All the marketing and other distribution decisions are made in-house. The division sends out promotional and advertising materials, arranges screenings of films, and makes deals with domestic and foreign distributors. Because of their size and the quantity of completed films each year, the studios naturally have a lot of clout in getting their films onto theater screens.

For the foreign markets, studios have offices around the world either singly or with other studios, to distribute their films in other countries. Often, a studio will partner with a local distributor, and the release will bear the names of both companies. The studio always retains the copyright, which it licenses to the foreign distributor for a specific length of time.

Based on the formulas we saw in Chapter 4, the studio's distribution arm receives its share of the box office grosses from the exhibitor and passes them through the accounting systems. The studio charges distribution fees back against the film as if its distribution division were a separate company. These fees can range from 30 to 40 percent of the total film rentals. In addition, the studio takes the entire fixed cost of the distribution division (overhead) and applies a portion of it to each film.

These overhead fees pay for running the division and cover expenses that are not covered by other fees. Before the accounting day is done, the studio will also take a portion of the overhead from the production side of the studio and add it to the total cost of the film.

The formula in Table 4.1 shows a "net profit" model for a studio film. Each studio has a standard method in its contracts for determining revenues, expenses, and profits. These formulas are nearly impossible to change, even by influential filmmakers. Typically, the producer has a percentage of the net profits in addition to receiving a salary. With studio films, it is fair to say that the chances of the net profit being greater than zero is rarer than with independent films. The studios have more films to cross-collateralize (using the profits from one film to offset the losses from another) and more places to bury unreasonable cost, although many contracts now prohibit films from being cross-collateralized.

The Advantages

There are many advantages to studio distribution. The studio has the ability to put 3,000 prints of one film in circulation on opening weekend. Its own channels of distribution are manifold. The studio has the financial resources to inundate television and the press with ads, and it have significant clout in getting placements for producers, directors, and actors on early-morning and late-night national interview shows.

As noted earlier, the studios have been able to monopolize the chain movie theaters in the past. Some have moved back into theater ownership. Be that as it may, with the success of independent films, exhibitors insist that they do not bow to studio pressure. They can only afford to have films in their houses that fill the theater seats. If the audience does not come to see a particular film, the exhibitor must look for another that will be more popular. With the success of independent films, exhibitors have made more theaters available for them. Recently, as small films have received acclaim, they have gone wide (in this case, 700–1,200 theaters) to major chains that would not have played them previously.

INDEPENDENT DISTRIBUTION

The Players, They Are A-Changin'

Four years ago, neither your author nor Bob Dylan could have foreseen what would be going on. Then, many would-be seers thought the independents would disappear. During the past few years, studios have realized the quickest entry to the independent market is to buy the companies (or in the case of Sony Classics, the people) who have done it. They may change their home address, but not much else. And as this book goes to press, several companies are in play.

Companies that were new or expanding in 1993 have become more highly capitalized. For example, October Films released its first film, *Life Is Sweet*, in 1991. The company was formed in March of the same year. By 1993, the company had completed a private placement, taken in other equity partners, and expanded its ability to market and exploit its films. With multiple Academy Award nominations in 1996 for *Secrets and Lies* and *Breaking the Waves*, the company is recognized as a major player. Universal, having sold its 50 percent of Gramercy back to Polygram, needs a specialty division. Universal Pictures bought a majority interest in October Films in April 1997. At the same time, a consortium headed by investment firms Bain Capital and Richland, Gordon & Company bought Live Entertainment, said to have one of the largest independent film libraries (2,000 titles) in the world, for $93 million. Several executives played musical chairs from Miramax to October to Live after the two acquisitions. Originally desiring to buy three companies—October, Live, and Trimark—Bain et al. was looking at the film libraries of Trimark and CiBy 2000 for possible purchase the following summer. The story doesn't end there. By the time you read this book, you will have updates to make to this particular script.

This acquisition mania only gives credence to the health of the independent group as a whole. The movement of New Line into the mega-corporation arena only leaves the field open for more of the small independents to increase their own market share. Companies such as Overseas FilmGroup, Image, Strand, Manga, Northern Arts, Cabin Fever, Unapix, and BMG are a few among the many. In the past few years Canadian companies Cinepix Film Properties (CFP) and Malo have been distributing films in the U.S. CFP recently acquired *Sunday*, which won the 1997 Sundance Dramatic Film Grand Jury Prize and the Waldo Salt Screenwriting Award for U.S. distribution. As they do this and obtain more profit, their resources increase for marketing films.

The entire universe of independent film is almost impossible to measure. We can assume that independent distributors are not releasing studio films. On the other hand, many independently financed features are released by studios, and when a studio releases a film, the source of the production financing is often not publicly known. The activity of independent distributors, therefore, is the best measure we have for independent movies. Since the landscape is constantly changing in this dynamic industry, the independent filmmaker must function in a fluid environment. The small independent of today could be the Miramax of tomorrow.

When writing your proposal, you have to decide which group of numbers tells your story best. The most recent data may be a year or two behind because of the flow of revenues. You therefore have the opportunity to forecast to the current period, putting whatever spin on these statistics you feel is justified. Your description of independent distribution should involve more than just how many films there were and how much money they took in as a group. Your goal is to show that the independent film market is healthy and that profits have nowhere to go but up.

How It Works

Watching the independent distributor at work takes in all the possible roles performed by the distributor. More than just a functionary for getting your picture out, the independent distributor can perform one or more other roles, including participating in creative decisions and contributing to the film's financial resources. For most independent filmmakers, the independent distributor is the only game in town and deserves an extensive look.

Domestic versus Foreign

The domestic territory generally comprises just the United States, but it might also be considered to include Canada and, many times, Puerto Rico and other Caribbean islands. Many of the independent distributors consider the United States and Canada to be one package and prefer not to have them separated beforehand. For one thing, the distributor may have output deals with Canada. If the opportunity for Canadian financing arises, therefore, producers must be careful. If the Canadian investors are going to take some or all of the Canadian territory for themselves, the producer might have a problem finding a distributor for the U.S. market. Before signing such an agreement, therefore, it is best to investigate the possibilities of finding a willing domestic distributor.

Domestic rights refer not only to theatrical distribution but to all the other media such as video, cable, and television. A producer who secures an advance from one of these media for production financing makes the deal a little less attractive to the distributor by fractionalizing the rights. Any source of future revenue taken out of the potential money pie makes the distribution deal tougher for the producer to close. Most distributors make a substantial investment in print and advertising costs. Although they may recoup these amounts from the theatrical marketplace, it is not likely to cover their distribution fees. Therefore, they prefer that other revenue sources be available to them.

Being a domestic distributor usually means that a company does not sell foreign rights themselves. Miramax started as a domestic distributor. The company's purchases of *The Crying Game* and *Strictly Ballroom*, for example, involved only domestic distribution. October Films, Strand Releasing, Fine Line, and First Look Pictures (domestic division of foreign sales company Overseas Filmgroup) are other domestic distributors. However, no rule says that a domestic distributor cannot venture into foreign waters. When Miramax lost its bid to distribute *Shine* in the U.S., it picked up the foreign rights. In addition, any company will probably be willing to be a one-stop shop for you. For example, a domestic distributor can certainly arrange a deal for you with a foreign sales distributor, and vice versa. On the other hand, keep in mind that the more participants in a deal, the more fees are subtracted from it.

On the foreign sales side, there are U.S.-based distributors specializing in the nondomestic market. These companies deal with networks of subdistributors all around the world. It is sometimes confusing for producers to distinguish between a distributor and a foreign sales agent. If a distribution company is granted the rights to the film for the foreign markets, that company is the distributor. Generally, if the producer retains ownership of the foreign rights and only grants someone a percentage of the receipts for obtaining distribution contracts for a particular territory and/or medium, then that person is a sales agent. The *Hollywood Distributors Directory* is a good reference for both domestic and foreign distributors. Also, AFMA publishes an annual directory of their members.

A Deal Is a Deal

What is a typical deal? There is no such animal; no two deals are ever exactly the same. Distributors will take as much as they can get, and it is the producer's job to give away as little as possible. This amount can be as low as 15 percent (for a "hired gun") or as high as 50 percent of the revenues from the film. Although most companies treat domestic and foreign revenues separately, industry averages are 32–35 percent unless you have a distribution contract in hand. Because no two deals are alike, the parameters discussed here are ballpark estimates and should not be used as a litmus test for the distributor. And as I will keep repeating, negotiating these percentages is reason to have an attorney experienced with film deals.

How much the distributor wants to take depends on the company's participation in the entire film package. The distributor may

- Get a finished picture
- Provide print and advertising (P&A) money
- Be rented
- Raise equity or presale financing
- Provide a minimum guarantee
- Pay an advance

There are no hard and fast rules. A lot depends on how much risk the distributor is taking and, in the last analysis, how badly the company wants the film. The amount of risk is primarily related to the amount of money the distribution company pays out of its pocket. The more up-front expenses it has to assume, the greater the percentage of incoming revenues it will seek. These percentages apply only to the revenues generated by the distributor's own deals; if that company is only making foreign sales for you, then it takes a percentage of foreign revenues only.

Be careful about assuming knowledge about another film's agreement and promising the same deal to your investor. Recently, a client wanted me to give examples of purchase prices in his business plan. For example, the trades say that Fine Line bought the U.S. domestic rights for *Shine* for $2.5 million. But we do not know if this was a total buyout or if there is a gross revenue amount over which more money will be returned to the producers, etc. You also have to keep track of whether the money bought rights to the entire world, a few countries, or one country. Sometimes a producer or director will give details in an interview. For example, Miramax paid $5 million for *Swingers* ($250,000 budget). According to director Doug Liman, who gave several in-depth interviews, of that amount, approximately $750,000 paid deferments and $1 million was paid in commissions to agencies, leaving an apparent $3 million for the producers and equity investors.

Prints and Ads Money

The first step in distributing a film is making copies of it. Prints are copies made from the master print, which is made from the original edited negative. For all intents and purposes, the print is the specific motion picture release, as the master does not circulate. It is kept in a vault for safekeeping and used when additional prints are necessary. One print usually costs $1,200 to $1,500, depending on the length of the film and current film stock costs. A wide distribution can cost well over $3 million for prints alone. Independent distributors, who have much smaller budgets than studios, usually start with only a few prints—sometimes even one.

Many distributors encourage producers to provide the P&A money, because this limits their risk even more. Producers who do provide the P&A can negotiate a lower distribution fee, often ranging from 10 to 22.5 percent, with the most common fees being 15 to 17.5 percent. These deals—often called "Rent-a-Distributor" or "Hired Gun"—usually have an escalator clause to give the distributor an incentive. For example, the fee might be 15 percent until net revenues to the producer equal the cost of the film or some multiple of the cost of the film, at which time the distribution fees escalate to 17.5 percent. On the other hand, some distributors just negotiate a flat fee for working this way.

There are varied opinions on whether it is practical for a producer to pay P&A costs. By putting up the money, the producer lessens the amount that the distributor will receive from the total revenues. On the other hand, many believe that the greater the distributor's share of the incoming revenues, the harder the company will work to maximize them. The producer may also be cast in the role of monitoring the value of the distribution process; without experience, how will you be able to judge? How to handle the P&A questions is one you have to decide for yourself. In the end, however, having to ask an investor for several million dollars in addition to the production costs may help you decide to forego this choice.

Distributor as Financier

Chapter 7 discusses financing in detail, but let's look here at the situation that arises when the distribution company is the provider of funds. If the distribution company produces a minimum guarantee, it is taking on greater risk, and therefore the fees are higher. Sometimes, the deal may give the distributor an equity participation in the film on the back end. The distribution fee is taken off the top, expense reimbursements are second, and then the revenues are split on some percentage basis. The distributor is now on the hook for providing a minimum amount of money no matter what the film does. If the company has provided a bankable guarantee for the producer, the distributor has to make good on the bank loan.

DISTRIBUTOR STRATEGIES

The marketing of the film to the general public is the distributor's job. The distributor makes decisions regarding the representation of the film in terms of genre, the placement of advertisements in various media, the sales approach for exhibitors and foreign buyers, and the "hype" (word of mouth, promotional events, alliances with special interest groups, and so on)—all of which are critical to a film's success.

Because marketing is part of the distribution company's area of expertise, it usually is unwilling to give the filmmaker a say in the sales strategy, the poster design, or how the film is portrayed. This comes as a shock to many filmmakers, who assume that they are going to have significant input or even a vote on how the posters look and where the film is opened. Many producers and directors expect a studio to ignore them, but they are under the impression that small distributors run their businesses as cooperative ventures.

Look at this from the distributor's point of view. Too many people involved in the decision-making process could be a nightmare. Formulating a marketing plan by committee could result in the proverbial camel. Artistic people tend to feel that they know the best way to present their project. After all, it is their baby, and they know it more intimately than anyone else. And how hard could advertising really be?

Franklin Delano Roosevelt said, "If I were starting life all over again, I would go into the advertising business; it has risen with ever-growing rapidity to the dignity of an art." We are all specialists, and marketing is the forte of the distributor. The filmmaker's task is to check out the distributor by researching other films the company has sold and the methods they used in the process. It is hoped that the distributor and the filmmaker will meet each other's standards and that a marriage will be made. Doing your own research to find the best distributor for you should head off a divorce later down the line.

What the Distributor Looks For

In acquiring a project, the distributor looks at many of the same elements discussed in Chapter 3:

- Uniqueness of storyline
- Genre
- Ability of the cast members to attract audiences or buyers on their names alone
- Past successes of the producers or director
- Name tie-in from another medium, such as a best-selling novel
- Special audience segment for the type, or genre, of film
- Attached money

Being able to sell a film involves a mix of elements, although the story is always the first concern. The people to whom the distributors sell must see something in the film that will appeal to their audiences. This varies from country to country and depends on the perspective of the buyer.

The perspective can change from distributor to distributor. No two are necessarily alike. It is difficult to define why one distributor will buy a particular film while the distributor in the next booth will not. It often boils down to a gut feeling—a notion that the distributor knows how to sell and profit from the movie. Every company operates in its own particular niche, but on a given day any distributor is liable to buy any film that appeals.

As a producer, you cannot count on miracles or on someone's gut feelings, however. Your best bet is to make your product and your approach as strong as possible. The more components that you bring to the table with the film, the more ammunition your distributor has. Negotiating is their business, but they need something with which to negotiate.

To complicate your life even more, the definition of a saleable commodity can change from year to year or from market to market. While distributors are in the thick of the battle getting the latest information, the rest of us might be a year behind. This situation makes meeting and talking to distributors crucial. One year, for example, I arrived at the American Film Market to promote a client's already finished film. The director convinced a well-known actress to do a 15-minute wraparound. She had been popular at previous markets. Unfortunately, the most recent European market had seen a glut of films with this person, and when I arrived at the American Film Market to make my pitch, there were yawns all around. The distributors knew because that is their business. We had not thought to check in and see if the star's popularity had changed.

Presales are another area that filmmakers often assume (and include in their business plans) as a given. However, you cannot count on such a sale until the deal has been completed. For example, when a film called *The Soldier's Wife* appeared at the 1992 American Film Market looking for presales, it already had experienced elements attached. Each of these elements was known in some markets, but not all; the American population was not familiar with the British stars (this was before Miramax's advertising blitz for the completed film). In addition, no one wanted to take a chance on the script at that time. When the film was eventually made and released, those elements were still attached, and the title was changed to *The Crying Game*. At what point the "secret" was included is not clear. Eventually, a consortium of British Screen Finance, Nippon Film Development, and Channel Four (from Britain) provided the financing. The rest of the world had to see it to believe it.

Approaching a distribution company with a finished film has advantages, of course. Then the distributor knows what you can do and how it will look on the screen. The company's risk level is lowered, and its financial output is less. A finished film also puts you in a stronger negotiating position. Many distributors say that they prefer even partially completed films to scripts because they feel that there is less chance of being sued for stealing someone's film.

Festivals are another way to secure distribution. If you can get your film accepted at one of the primary festivals (Sundance, Toronto, Cannes), you have a chance of attracting distribution. Individually, those festivals tend to attract more distributors than all other U.S. festivals. Being at a competitive festival is good. You will find the psychology of the herd at work. If an audience likes a film or if one distributor becomes interested, all of a sudden a distributor feeding frenzy can start and prices go up.

Methods for Releasing Films

No one invents new release strategies; they just refine the old tried and true ones over time. Some are in fashion, and some are out of fashion, but there are basically only a few ways to release a film. When Peter Myers was senior vice president of Twentieth Century Fox Entertainment, he wrote,

Basically, there are two release patterns for motion pictures: fast and slow. The fast pattern is for any well-known or easily exploitable subject that lends itself to a massive television advertising campaign. The slow pattern is for a more sensitive picture, without presold ingredients, which would require a gradual familiarizing of the public through favorable reviews and articles and the deliberate spreading of word of mouth.[2]

Myers said it all in a nutshell. All of the distribution books that you read (and you should learn as much as you can) will give names to procedures that are variations of fast and slow.

Fast

The fastest way to release a film is to release it wide. Studios use this strategy for releasing many of their films. A thousand or more prints open simultaneously around the country. For example, *Independence Day* opened on 2,882 screens and *Twister* on 2,414 screens. It used to be that you needed stars to open a film. Lately, special effects are the stars in many big budget films. *Mission Impossible* with Tom Cruise opened on 3,012 screens but did not gross as well as the other two films.

The wide release allows for a big opening weekend, which could have one of two outcomes. First, suppose a lot of people go to see the film, like it, and tell their friends. Assuming that the film opens on 2,000 screens, the average mall theater seats around 500 people, and the film shows three times a day, you have around a million people leaving the theater on a Saturday and telling their friends to see the film. The film develops excellent "legs," which means that it runs for a long time with good box office. The studios often use the results of the opening weekend as a measure of what the total domestic box office will be.

The second possible result of a big weekend is that the same people leave the theater and tell their friends, "Don't go see that turkey." The film doesn't have legs. It does have the advantage, however, of many people coming to the theater the first few weekends to see the star, so the studio can advertise the large weekend grosses to lure more moviegoers into the theaters before they hear any bad word of mouth.

[2]Jason E. Squire, ed., *The Movie Business Book* (p. 277). New York: Simon & Schuster, 1983.

Moderate Speed

In several standard patterns of release, a film opens in more than one theater at a time but in fewer than 500 overall. The standard definition for an independent used to be one that opened in 475 theaters or less. Saturation, platform, rollout, and sequencing are variations on this theme. The film starts in a few selected theaters and moves on in some sort of pattern. A particular film may work best in one market because of the makeup of the population, because the film was shot there, or because the locals will go to see almost anything.

Films with difficult themes or at least an unknown audience may open in New York City or Los Angeles. The cosmopolitan nature and size of the populations in those cities are an advantage. If a borderline film is destined to find any commercial acceptance, it will be in one of those towns. With good reviews, the film will continue to move through the country in one of several fashions. It might move to contiguous states, open in successive theaters based on a certain schedule, or cascade into the markets that are most likely to produce revenue. Whatever method is used, the film will continue to open in more and more theaters. Eventually, the number of theaters will decrease, but the film will remain in distribution as long as it attracts audiences.

These methods have several advantages. They give unique films special handling, and they allow a popular-genre, small-budget film to move at the limit of its advertising budget. For example, if your film has a sensitive Native American theme, you can open in a moderately large city that also has a significant Native American population, such as Seattle. In this instance, the film plays to a special-interest audience in a town where the initial box office dollars probably will give you a good start.

The goal of moderate-speed distribution is to realize sizable opening audiences (relative to the budget and theme of the film) and good reviews, then use the money and reviews to continue distribution. Clearly, no one expects a $3-million film to sell $17 or $20 million in tickets during the first weekend. The distributor may start with a few prints and fund the copying of more out of the revenues from the first few theaters. Advertising works the same way. Ads in a major city newspaper can run anywhere from $1,000 to $10,000. As a moderately budgeted film earns money, it finances the advertising in the cities to come.

Leaving Las Vegas opened on 7 screens and gradually expanded to 527 screens. The film, with a budget of $4.7 million, grossed $32 million in the U.S. Admittedly, having Nicolas Cage star was a help; nevertheless, a film in which the lead dies can often die at the box office. Had word of mouth not been good and had the audiences failed to grow, it is unlikely that the distributor (MGM/UA) would have extended the run as long as it did.

Slow

The difference between slow and moderate-speed distribution is not necessarily the type of sequencing, but the budget of the distributor. A very small distribution company may only be able to afford one print. Therefore, the film will start in one theater and move ahead at the same speed, perhaps getting to a total of five to 20 theaters, for its entire run. Low-budget (or "no-budget," as some are called) films are promoted with this kind of marketing budget—exceedingly small.

"Four-walling" is another tactic that sometimes works with lower-budget films. In this case, the distributor rents a theater for a flat weekly fee and takes all the receipts. The gamble is that the total box office dollars will be significantly greater than the guaranteed minimum to the exhibitor. Four-walling is used infrequently now, although occasionally a producer will revive it.

Another option is self distribution. Sometimes filmmakers have no choice and must implement a variation of these two methods by themselves. Some filmmakers state with a certain bravado in their business plans, "We will look for distribution. But if we don't find it, we'll distribute the film ourselves." I have seen this not only with first-time $500,000 films but also in packages looking for $8 or $9 million. Before choosing this course, think long and hard.

Many producers have been successful at distributing their first films. If you speak with them afterward, however, they usually say they would not want to do it a second time. Self-distribution usually is done out of necessity because no distributor will pick up the product. No one knows how much more successful the film would have been with an experienced distributor. Self-distribution carries a big risk for the producer, and a lack of skill can be dangerous.

Not to belabor a point made earlier, but distributors have a body of experience, knowledge, and relationships that are hard to beat. If you think it is tricky to negotiate with one distributor, try negotiating with 30 in as many countries. The international market is a different deal in every country. You have to know how to structure the deals, what the censorship rules are, how you are going to get the money out of the country, and how to set up the mechanism to deliver the film. At the very least, an individual should try to work in concert with a producer's representative to ease some of the complications.

Domestic distribution is not necessarily a picnic, either. The exhibitors have been in business a long time and are experienced negotiators. To check the receipts, you may have to stand at the box office and count the "house" as people buy tickets. Many filmmakers have taken a small film to a local specialty theater or two and shown that they can attract an audience. Then they are able to make a deal with a distribution company to take the film to more theaters. An example is *Claire of the Moon*. The producer released the lesbian-themed film in a few theaters in San Francisco and then was able to make a deal with Strand Releasing to more theaters.

The 90/10 deal is a booking procedure that goes hand in hand with the release of small films. The distributor makes a deal with the theater to put up 90 percent of the advertising money and take 90 percent of the gross, after the exhibitor takes an agreed-upon minimum guarantee to earn the house "nut." This type of deal could be done at other percentages, but 90/10 is common. Distributors always try to negotiate the best deals they can get and afford.

FILMMAKER STRATEGIES

David versus Goliath

Many filmmakers let fate determine which way they will go in terms of distribution: studio or independent. This decision has no right or wrong answers—only options. The studio brings with it deep pockets, backup advice from experienced producers, strong marketing, and the ability to retain screens. Independent distributors bring an intimate knowledge of the low-budget market, the ability to disseminate films carefully over time, and a willingness to take a chance. Weigh your options carefully before making a decision.

There is a certain wisdom to the thought, "Just get the film made." The hardest part of movie-making is making the first one.

Filmmakers often end up trying to decide whether to accept the only offer they get or trying to make a decision among a group of unfavorable deals. Although there are many concerns to be weighed in making a decision, you may have to be willing to make concessions on the first project.

One filmmaker's meat is another's poison. Before going into any negotiations, be clear on your goals. The distribution decision is the major reason that you went through the exercise of listing your wants and desires in the second chapter. You may seek advice and counsel from others, but in the end, you must make your own decisions. Table 6.1 will help you identify the pros and cons of studio and independent distribution.

The studio's backup system is a safety net for the new filmmaker. There are experienced producers and directors on the lot who can be dispatched to location. This might be an advantage or a disadvantage. The independent filmmaker, on the other hand, usually completes the film before finding a distributor and thus has far more freedom during the filmmaking process. Distributors generally do not have extra people to hang around the set and tell you how to direct or produce.

The nature of independent distribution supports smaller-budget films. In the studios, it is hard to make a film with a smaller budget. They've got unions, overhead, and extra costs galore. Independent distributors have to run a tighter ship. Certainly, when looking for financing, their goal is a small budget. The size of budgets for studio films usually leads to less imaginative and less chancy films being made. The independent system, meanwhile, embraces new and eclectic films. Studios maintain large bureaucracies, which make

Table 6.1 Pros and Cons: Studio versus Independent Distribution

	Studio	Independent
Backup	A lot	A little
Budgets	$15 million plus	$7,000 plus
Up-front Money	Generous	Little
Types of Films	Homogenized	Eclectic
Overrun Financing	Yes	No
Distribution Cutoff	Quick	Moderate
Bureaucracy	Heavy	Thin
Acquisitions	Sometimes	Preferred
Net Profit	Seldom	Sometimes
Producer's Control	None	Some

reaching a decision very difficult and time-consuming. The less cumbersome independent process enables quicker decisions because there are fewer hands in the pot.

The studio's financial resources generally favor generous salaries for producers, directors, and cast. With independent films, above-the-line money is often cut to lower the budget and make it doable. Most studios assume a certain level of budget overrun with pictures and have the resources to support it. Conversely, private equity investors expect the budget you give them to be the final number. Underestimating can be dangerous because investors may not make up the shortfall. (More on this subject in the next chapter.)

Studio distribution, as we have seen, is generally "get 'em out fast and wide." Historically, the studios have had neither the time nor the inclination to pamper a film through its release. It goes out everywhere with a lot of publicity. In addition, the studios have a short attention span. Films that fail to find their audiences quickly enough are pulled. Independent distributors, on the other hand, often have the knowledge and patience to give special care to eclectic or mixed-genre films. Many are geared to let a film find its audience slowly and methodically. Of course, there are some independent distributors whose forte is the mass-appeal genres. Most independents, though, have an expertise for releasing films with smaller budgets and lesser names.

The studios' desire to share in the small-film market usually lasts for only a brief time. Studios might go through cycles of acquiring smaller films, but independents are always there; this niche is their business. As we have seen, the reports of the death of independent distribution have been greatly exaggerated.

Earlier, we noted that your chances of a net profit on a studio film are low. There is a greater chance of having a real net profit at the end of the day with an independent film, although it is not guaranteed. The best policy in the movie business usually is to get what you can in the beginning—just in case.

The Control Factor

Filmmakers are well aware of the fact that studios retain the right to change anything they please—title, director's cut, and so on—and they assume that independent distributors will not want control over these things. They are wrong. All distributors want to control the title and the cut. The only way to have total control over your film is to finance and distribute it yourself.

With the studios, the filmmaker's lack of control over projects is the stuff of which legends are made. Once your project goes into the system, it may be the last time you see it. If you are the writer, the finished picture may bear little resemblance to your original.

Normally, there is far more control in independent filmmaking, but absolute control is a myth. An independent distributor will not allow you to have your way with everything. Novice filmmakers often are surprised at their lack of control. If only to protect themselves, distributors feel that they need these rights. Their biggest concern is to have a salable product, and, especially with neophyte producers and directors, they have no idea what they may be getting. A film that is too long, that drags in various places, or that includes scenes that were not approved in the original script will be a problem.

Most independent distributors would rather deal with a finished film. That way, they know what they are getting before making an agreement, and they can request certain changes before obtaining the film. Of course, turning over a finished film is no guarantee for the filmmaker that no changes will be made.

Be Aware

When going into a distribution negotiation meeting, know what items are important to you. Talk to your attorney and get a feel for the deal-breakers—that is, the points on which you will not negotiate. No matter what someone says to you verbally, written agreements are what count. For example, if having a hand in the marketing is important to you, have it included in the contract. Be advised that many distributors will not want to concede this item. This does not mean that they will not listen to your input, but they want the final say.

Learn from the experiences of others. One novice filmmaker sent his distributor 40 minutes of finished film and 45 minutes of dailies. Although they had said that they wouldn't change a frame, they used the dailies to change the film to meet their standards. In addition, they took a frame from a scene that was not in the finished film to use for the poster. This allowed the distributor to promote the film as belonging to a different genre than it actually did. Will the average distributor do this? Probably not, but it is your responsibility to check out the people you will be dealing with to see how they have handled other filmmakers' projects.

In the last analysis, you must enter into the distribution agreement with care. Make sure your rights are spelled out. If you see the term "standard agreement," ask for a definition. Finally—and this cannot be said too strongly or too often—get a film attorney's advice before signing anything. I used to just say "entertainment attorney." But you need an attorney with experience in your industry. Whether it is film, television, music, book publishing, multimedia, or some other area, be sure that your attorney has experience specific to your needs.

WHAT DO YOU TELL INVESTORS?

The salient facts are here, but you must decide how much explanation to include. Always keep your description short and to the point. The distribution section of your business plan should run four or five pages at most.

On the other hand, do say something useful. Your investors may know even less than you about distribution; as with other subjects, you have to dispel any wrong impressions they might have. Many investors think that their production financing gives them control of the distributor, too. In addition, some have been known to assume that the distributor will repay them all the production costs up front before the film is released. These notions may prevent you from finding a distributor; in that case, no one will ever see your film.

Before you propose to take charge of all the marketing and promotion strategies yourself or decide to self-distribute your films, ask yourself a question: Who is going to make decisions? The idea may sound great—it will give you control—but there may well be pitfalls. If you do not know how to drive a car, what do you do after you turn on the ignition?

Getting a distribution deal is never a given. If you leave investors with the impression that it automatically comes with making the film, you may end up with a bigger problem than you ever imagined. I have seen many business plans that have a single statement—"We will get a distributor"—as the entire distribution section. As you should realize by now, this approach is not the best. Do your research before writing your plan and explain the essentials. Then you will be in good shape to give investors confidence in your ability and your knowledge.

7

Financing

*Where large sums of money are concerned, it is advisable to
trust nobody.*

AGATHA CHRISTIE
Endless Night, Book II

Shuffle a pack of playing cards. Now spread them out face down, and
pick one card. If it is the ace of spades, you win; if it is not, you lose.
Your chances here are one out of 52 of getting the right card. These
odds are better than the odds of finding independent money for your
film. Do not be discouraged, though. Many filmmakers face these
odds each year—and win.

Film is probably the worst investment anyone could ever make.
It is unsafe, unreliable, and generally unbelievable. If risks were measured on a scale of 1 to 10, movies would rate a 15. One might as well
go to Las Vegas and throw the dice—in fact, those odds are probably
better. Why would anyone invest in films, then? From a purely
financial standpoint, it is a gamble for which there is a big payoff. In
addition, there are many subjective reasons for investing in films such
as personal ideals, creative participation, and being part of the glitter
and glamour. The specific people and firms that are likely to fund
films change, but the modus operandi remains the same. Some of the
different sources of financing will be relevant for your situation;
others will not. Some are dynamic; some are static. As studio executives and production companies go through cycles, so do forms of
financing.

By this point, you are well on your way to a finished proposal. You have explained the basic information—your company and product, the industry, the market, and the distribution process. You have your goals and objectives well in hand. Now here is the kicker. Popular agent lore (spread by agents) is that if a script is not interesting after the first 10 minutes, it gets thrown in the "forget it" pile. Something similar can be said of investors and business plans. Investors typically read the Executive Summary first and the Financial Section second. If they are still interested, they read all the delicious text between the two. This does not mean that all the in-between material is irrelevant, just that the primary emphasis is on the ins and outs of financing and how the numbers look.

When thinking about investors, most people picture a singularly rich person who swoops in and says, "Here's an extra $10 million I found in my drawer. Go make a film—no strings attached." Or, a country suddenly passes a law guaranteeing you 100 percent of your film costs just for showing up. This is the stuff of which movie plots are made. Not an impossible scenario, but an improbable one. You may get lucky early on, but it is more likely that there will be false starts, dashed hopes, and months or years of frustration.

As the saying goes, "If it were easy, everyone would be doing it." The truth is that finding financing is hard work. If you think otherwise, forget it. There are almost as many ways to finance a movie as there are people reading this book. We will look at specific methods, but note that the full financing of your movie may be a combination of several methods.

With a business plan for a new company, there is an additional struggle. Whether you are asking a money source to invest in one film or several, creating a feeling of confidence is not easy. Any anxiety on the part of the investor about funding one of your films is magnified when committing to finance an entire company. Besides making successful films, you have to be able to run that company. The investor will be looking with great care, therefore, at the management staff.

In your financing section, you will discuss how your films will find financing, but you should do this without restating this entire chapter. Only certain financial strategies will be appropriate for your particular projects or for the type of investor you are going after. Too much irrelevant information will only confuse your reader.

This chapter examines some of the specific sources of money: single investors (rich people), presales, co-production and below-the-line deals, negative pickups, and limited partnerships. In addition, it takes a brief look at bank loans. This chapter is meant to give you a general knowledge of how film financing works; the intention is to make a complex subject easy to understand and to give you material for your business plan. It is not meant to be the complete and final word on the subject. For your own knowledge, do additional research on the specific financing techniques that you plan to use.

BEFORE YOU START

Before writing the finance section of your business plan, there are several guidelines to think about and to follow. These concern the following:

- Seeking reality
- Finding the best fit
- Being careful what you promise
- Being careful what they promise
- Being able to explain it

Seeking Reality

The way that one person financed a film yesterday may not be relevant to you today. This appears to go against what was said earlier about learning from other filmmakers, but it does not. We said it was sometimes the same formula, not necessarily the same people. For example, suppose a filmmaker moves to Cincinnati, goes to play miniature golf, and meets a corporate executive. That very day, the corporation had decided to finance a film, so a deal is struck. That corporation may never fund another film. In fact, no one in Cincinnati may ever fund another film. Do not assume that you will find money in the same place. Learn from the other filmmaker's method, however; it may prove useful for you.

Finding the Best Fit

Filmmakers often believe that all money is equal; it isn't. Each source sets different requirements or conditions for the delivery of funds. You will be able to live with some of these; some not. For example, there may be too many hands in the pot. Three intermediaries later, you will be paying out huge sums. Or, prospective investors may have requirements that make getting the money not worthwhile. There may be content, length of time, or rate of return demands you cannot meet. Worse, at the eleventh hour, Ms. Investor may inform you that her husband has to play the lead in the film. Don't be discouraged. The right source for you is out there somewhere; seek until you find.

Being Careful What You Promise

Making statements of absolute fact about financial conditions may be dangerous. An investor will hold you to whatever you promise. You might say, for example, "We will seek presales in order to recover at least some of the production financing up front." That is not a promise, only a statement of intent. On the other hand, saying to people, "We will obtain presale commitments," is a promise. Unless you have commitments already in hand, you may be making a promise that you cannot keep. And be careful of implied promises. If you want to tell them the purchase prices of *The Spitfire Grill* or *Sling Blade*, be sure to say these prices are unusual. I have seen investors refuse to approve a distribution deal because they assumed "normal" purchases were for twice the negative cost of the film.

Being Careful What They Promise

Always take the stance that you have to see it to believe it. People do not have to be con artists to lead you astray; many just like to hear themselves talk. Even investment bankers are seen bragging at cocktail parties about films they never financed. Whether a money source (finder or actual) is saying, "The check is in the mail," or promising money-back guarantees, check the paperwork. If you are not knowledgeable about financial terms and clauses, find someone who is. Your mantra should be, "Do not spend any money until the cash is in the production account." This warning includes family friends and bank executives as well.

Being Able to Explain It

If you cannot explain a financing scheme, do not include it. To my constant amazement, I often receive business plans based on financing structures that the producer does not understand—and not just from inexperienced filmmakers. Longtime professionals will base entire companies on intricate currency methods they can't explain. Frankly, not only are many of these too complex for me, but a majority don't work. You can bet your bottom dollar that an investor will ask for details about the financing with examples of companies that have used them successfully, so be prepared.

RICH PEOPLE: THEM THAT HAS THE GOLD

Investors are both business people and gamblers. Film is one of the biggest gambles you can find, but individuals go for it all the time. Jim McIngvale, the Texas entrepreneur who financed *Sidekicks*, told the *Los Angeles Times*, "It's just like wildcatting oil in Texas, except I'm wildcatting motion pictures.... This is a pretty impressive roll of the dice."

Private investors are equity players. They take a portion of the net worth of your company in exchange for their capital. Until you take in partners, you own the whole pie. As partners come in, you start to slice the pie into little pieces, and as the old saying goes, "Them that has the gold, makes the rules." The nature of an entrepreneur is to be filled with a passion to accomplish a certain end. The hardest job for you may be your own emotional involvement, when attempting to see things from the investor's point of view.

Who Are They?

The first string of the investment team comprises friends and relatives. Raising development money and the negative costs of films under $1 million is very difficult. Professional investors do not see enough of a return on such small investments. Mom and Uncle Harry are more likely to be willing to give you a chance. Ed Burns raised the initial $20,000 for *The Brothers McMullen* with credit cards from family and friends. Kevin Smith funded the $26,575 budget for *Clerks* with credit-card advances, the sale of his comic book collection, and a loan from his parents.

Entrepreneurs

Private money comes most often from people in businesses other than entertainment. Entrepreneurial types who have made a killing in almost any industry may feel the lure of film. It takes a high roller at heart to start a firm and prosper with it. You can try the annual *Forbes 400* for a listing of billionaires; however, you may have to travel to Hong Kong or Taiwan to speak with them. You don't have to go that far.

Well-to-do owners of medium-size companies often have enough money to finance a small to moderate film. Several years ago a Cleveland furniture dealer sold his chain of showrooms and moved to Hollywood to get into the film business. Penelope Spheeris found him first, and he funded her first film, *Suburbia*. Jim McIngvale, also known as Mattress Mac, happened to be a Chuck Norris fan. He funded the entire budget and cost of prints and ads for Norris' *Sidekicks* for $16 million. Check out your local home furnishings giant, just in case.

Investors have all sorts of reasons for taking this risk. Betting on something one likes (e.g., karate, Jane Austen) and making a profit at the same time is worth a spin of the wheel of fortune. Seldom are investors seeking to lose money. I have seen scores of creative people forget their dreams rather than face the reality that, whatever the content, these are business deals as well.

Art

Some investors want to be associated with "art." To this day, people will tell me that they want to make *A Room with a View*. Unfortunately, they want to make it at 1986 prices and reap the box office of *Fargo* ($46 million worldwide so far). Merchant–Ivory Productions also would like to make *A Room with a View* for $1,000,000 today.

In such a case, the investor's goals are unrealistic. You should make an attempt to create realistic expectations for him. If you are lucky, his desire to be associated with quality will outweigh the high return he wants for his investment. On the other hand, if he cannot afford more money and does not want to join with additional investors, move on. Put your energy into finding partners whose outlook and resources are a match for your project.

Special Interests

The line between business and altruism can be a thin one. Few people will become involved in a feature film without considering its commercial possibilities, but investors often have other reasons for funding. If you can find an investor whose sensibilities agree with a special interest of your film, you may be able to create a workable collaboration.

Despite Spike Lee's considerable success and the substantial success of African-American films, he could not convince a studio to back *Get On the Bus*, a $2 million film about people on a bus traveling to the Million Man March to Washington. Finally, he went to 15 African-American entrepreneurs and celebrities to raise the money. In the past, I have had students or clients take umbrage with such an idea. Here is a famous writer–director going to the people with a subjective interest in seeing the film made.

And don't forget nonprofit organizations. *The Spitfire Grill* was written to meet the needs of the Mississippi-based Sacred Heart League, a Roman Catholic charity, looking to invest money in a "spiritually uplifting" film. The film premiered at the 1996 Sundance Film Festival, where Castle Rock acquired the $6.1 million project for a surprising $10 million. The backers were happy. The film delivered their message and an immediate profit at the same time. Many foundations and similar organizations have funded all or part of documentaries or feature films that fit with their particular mandate.

Foreign Investors

We hear a lot about European and Japanese investment in the American film community. In the early to mid-90s, most of the foreign money went to studios or the formation of large production companies with experienced studio executives; $100 million was a favorite startup amount. Very little went to small films by novice filmmakers.

There is always an exception to every rule. In 1992, a Japanese company, Tokuma Communications, funded five new directors with $250,000 each. One of the films from that program, *Public Access*, directed by Bryan Singer, shared a Grand Jury prize at the 1993 Sundance Film Festival. Singer's next film, for an American company, was *The Usual Suspects*; and the rest, as they say in filmland, is history. Unfortunately, that particular program was canceled after its first year. In the past two or three years, however, more foreign companies have been opening Los Angeles or New York offices to stick their toes in the water. There is a lot of competition for these dollars, but individual filmmakers have managed to make the right connection.

In tracking foreign money, you often run into "finders," people claiming to have a special relationship with foreign money. Some do; many do not. Remember to check these people out and *do not give them any money in advance.* A finder should be paid a percentage of the money you receive from the investor, and only after the cash is in your bank account.

Where Are They?

Your own backyard is the first place to look for financing. Few film-makers are born in Los Angeles; they migrate there. Nor are the investors born in Los Angeles. They are born and live in Ohio, Michigan, Iowa, Texas, Maui, Florida, and so on. At least, those are areas where many of my clients have found investors. (Don't call me for a list; it's proprietary—nonpublic, company-owned—infor-mation.) You may find untapped markets of entrepreneurs with lots of money from very boring industries, to whom the lure of the film world may be irresistible. Your best chance is in an area where there is not a lot of competition from other filmmakers—if there still is such a place. The entire financing deal can be conducted without anyone living in Tinsel Town; however, be sure to work with an attorney with film experience.

If all else fails, give a party. Sometimes the way to get potential investors to a meeting is to arrange an evening for charity or just plain fun that includes a star or stars the investors admire. Theater pro-ducers do this as a matter of course for their "angels," and it may be a route for you to take as well.

You may be surprised as to which third-string player in your film will be exciting for your particular group to meet.

What You Get

Equity investors will want at least a 50 percent cut of the producer's share in the film; some may even want a higher percentage. No matter how many years you spent writing the scripts or how many hours you spent talking deals, it is their money. The 50/50 split is usually one of those "gold" rules. Before you start complaining, be glad your investors don't want 80 percent. Venture capital companies and pro-fessional film investors often require that much equity to put seed money into a company.

Before any profit splits occur, investors must be paid back for their investments. Many investors will allow a 90/10 split (in their favor) until that sum is repaid. They want to keep you alive in case there is reason for a second film. However, I have seen not just strangers but relatives as well insist on a 100 percent payback with interest before the filmmaker receives a penny. After the distributor and the investor are repaid, the producer's share begins—50 percent of the net profit, one would hope.

Filmmakers have a habit of promising "points" and film credits to people for their work in finding investors or getting the project made. Directors who are too expensive for the film's budget often are given points as a deferment of part of their salary. These points all come out of the filmmaker's 50 percent. Investors are not responsible for any of these agreements unless they negotiated them. Besides points, filmmakers like to give away credits. Be careful what you promise. Only a handful of investors want to remain anonymous; the majority want to see their name on the screen, and their credit of choice is Executive Producer. If you are going to look for investors, reserve this card.

Reasonable Risk

Entrepreneurs often want money from investors with no strings attached as a reward for their creative genius. They do not want to be responsible for how the money is spent or for whether investors realize a gain. No doubt, you are a genius. But do not expect to get financing without showing the investor what kind of risk he is taking.

When I started in this business, a partner and I tried to get financing for an entrepreneur who had a new idea for using films for a specialized purpose in malls. One investor thought the project was "sexy" and that the idea could be taken national, but the business plan was so-so. The investor proposed to raise $5 million and look forward to a public offering (stock issue) for the new company. However, he wanted a revised business plan, and our client would have none of this. "After all," he said, "investors are supposed to take a risk. If these people are not willing to take one, who needs them? I'm not going to waste all this time. Big guys in New York are interested." You can probably guess what happened. The client never heard from the "big guys," never got his company funded, and went back to his old job, never to be heard from again.

The moral here is not that people in New York are unreliable. Serious investors, whether they are in New York or Des Moines, will seldom make a final decision based on flash and dash. They want to see substance and detail. Even if someone likes your project, chances are you will hear, "Come back when you have the paperwork."

The Big Payoff

The low-budget, big-return films are the hooks that lure many investors into the film business. Films like *Sling Blade* and *Four Weddings and a Funeral* will bring the high rollers into the financing arena. Very few other businesses, outside of Las Vegas, offer the potential of a 500 to 1,000 percent return on investment. As a filmmaker, you must be ready to show prospective investors that the chance of making a killing outweighs the risk of losing their money. Remember, though, that you can never promise a risk-free investment. And you do not want to tell them, "Ten million dollars is typical of advances and/or buyouts for $1 million films."

When all is said and done, it is the projected bottom line that builds the investor's confidence. You need to find similar films and track their dollar returns. Whether you are looking at a single film or a company, you must project your revenues and expenses, box office grosses and rentals, and cash flows over the next three to five years. (You will learn how to do that in the next chapter.)

PRESALES

The main activity at the markets—AFM, Cannes, MIFED—is seeking presales, or distributor commitments, for as-yet-unmade films in order to finance production. The seller (you or your U.S. distributor) approaches the buyer in each territory and medium (video, theatrical, satellite broadcast, and so on) to entice him or her to buy the ancillary rights (domestic or foreign) to your film in advance. (This is also called a "prebuy.") In return, you receive a commitment and guarantee from the prebuyers. The guarantee includes a promise from that company to pay a specific amount upon delivery of the completed film. If deemed credible by one of several specialized entertainment banks that accept such "paper," the contract can be banked. Then the bank will advance you a sum, minus their discount amount.

In exchange for the presale contract, the U.S. or foreign buyer obtains the right to keep the revenue (rentals) from that territory and might also seek equity participation. The agreement can be for a certain length of time, a revenue cap, or both.

The time period can be anywhere from 5 to 15 years, with 7 being customary. Many filmmakers are under the impression that "in perpetuity" (forever) enters into this negotiation. These terms are not unheard of, but they are more likely to surface if you are transferring the copyright, or ownership, of the film. There is nothing to keep people with money in their hands from demanding as much as they can get. The buyer tries to make the length of time as long as possible, and the seller tries to make it as short as possible. Be careful of the stance you take. Some foreign companies have told me that if the film-maker balks at 7 years, they will change the term to 10.

The "revenue cap" is a certain amount of money in sales, up to which the buyer gets to keep all the money. When negotiating these terms, buyers try to estimate the highest amount that the movie will make and then try to make that amount the cap. After the revenue cap is reached, the seller may start receiving a percent of the revenue or may renegotiate the deal.

Being the sole source of financing gives people much more power than if they are one of a group of funders. Yet any of these negotiations still depend on the "eye of the beholder." Any leverage depends on the desire of the buyer for the film.

Advances

Cable, home video, and television syndication companies have in the past been major sources of preproduction financing. Through advances, they fund all or part of a film's production in exchange for an equity participation and the rights to distribute the film in their particular medium. Although advances do not occur as frequently as they did three or four years ago, particularly in video, they are still a potential form of production financing. As noted earlier, though, most domestic distributors prefer not to see fractionalized rights. Always weigh this fact against the benefits of having an ancillary company as your main investor.

The advance for a finished film is another matter. It may be a total buyout, have a revenue cap, or combine any number of characteristics common to presales. When you see that Sony Classics, for example, has paid a certain price for the right to distribute a film, you do not know the parameters of the deal. Therefore, you want to be careful how you explain these deals to your potential investors.

Advantages and Disadvantages

The primary advantage of presales is that they offer you the chance to make your film. This source of money continues to be a workable one for new filmmakers. In addition, if you manage to reach your production goal over several territories, it lessens the impact that someone else can have on your film. Presumably, the fewer territories you presell or from which you receive advances, the more money you will be able to keep on the backend after distribution.

There are two disadvantages to this source of funding. First, you sacrifice future profits in order to make the film. Selling your film in advance puts you at a negotiating disadvantage. Companies that use presale strategies often give away much of the upside cash flow and profit potential from hit movies. Second, not all paper is bankable. You have to do a lot of research before accepting this kind of contract. Things change quickly, particularly in difficult economic times.

CO-PRODUCTION AND BELOW-THE-LINE DEALS

International co-production deals are the result of treaty agreements between countries. Qualifying films are permitted to benefit from various government incentives provided by the country in which production will take place. However, co-production agreements are not a charity event. A number of requirements may be imposed on the film by government treaty, including the following:

- The producer must be a resident of the host country.
- A certain percentage of above-the-line talent must come from the host country.
- A certain percentage of the technical crew must be residents of that country.
- Distribution must be done by a company located in the host country.
- A percentage of the revenues from the film must remain in that country.

Another type of co-production agreement can be made with various production facilities. Instead of providing hard cash (actual dollars with which to pay people), they provide studio time and equipment at large discounts or even free. Tied to these deals (and sometimes to the international arrangements), a company will provide below-the-line expenses ("soft currency") such as film stock, hotels, food, and the like.

Various U.S. states, cities, and privately owned studios have at some time offered co-production incentives. When studios were built in North and South Carolina, for example, their owners offered a break on studio and technical costs in order to attract business. At one time, Florida announced a program for supplying prints and ads money for independent films. The status of such deals is very fluid. By the time word spreads, the opportunity may be gone. These deals are shopped around the same way that scripts are, but they are always worth checking out.

Advantages and Disadvantages

The first advantage to co-production is that the total budget may be smaller because of the advantages of filming in a cheaper locale. Second, of the readjusted budget, you will have to find a smaller amount of hard cash. The right deal will cover most if not all of your below-the-line costs. Many films would still be only a gleam in the producer's eye if part of the actual cash burden had not been removed by a co-production deal.

In terms of disadvantages, you will still need to have hard cash for the above-the-line payroll—that is, the cast, director, writer, and production office staff. No film is made without these people, and they will not take I.O.U.s. Another disadvantage is that finding enough skilled personnel in a host country could be a problem. If you end up having to fly in technical people from the United States, you may end up with a budget burden that offsets the advantages of the co-production deal.

NEGATIVE PICKUP

In the days when film companies had more cash, there were many negative pickups. The premise is that a studio or distributor promises to pay the cost of the film negative (production costs) upon delivery of the completed picture. This agreement is taken to the bank, which then provides cash for production at a discount to the total value of the agreement. A discount is a reduction in the stated value of the note.

The Catch-22 here is that the bank has to believe that the studio or distributor will be able to pay off the loan upon delivery of the film (often a year from the date of the agreement). In the past, this was not as difficult to do as it is now. Four or five years ago, banks could count on the majors, a few of the mini-majors, and a very small number of distributors to make good on negative pickups. The entire situation has changed in the past several years. The financial problems of many of the large production companies are well known. In addition, the troubles and, in some cases, complete collapse of many financial institutions have created an even more dismal picture. Nothing can be taken for granted. The situation is a fluid one, and although there are still companies that will give you negative pickups, this is not a financing strategy that I would count on or promise to my investors.

Advantages and Disadvantages

One advantage of negative pickups is that the film is made without giving away a share of the company to someone else. In addition, a negative pickup with a major studio or distributor removes the angst of searching for a distributor.

On the other hand, the standard negative pickup agreement contains two loopholes that favor the distributor. First, the agreement has a built-in escape clause that says, in effect, "You must deliver the film we were promised." Any change in the script, even if it seems minor to you, can cause cancellation of the contract. Second, the contract also states that the finished film has to meet the distributor's standards of quality. Even if the movie is shot-for-shot the same as the script, the distributor can always say that the film's quality is not up to standards.

LIMITED PARTNERSHIPS

Until the mid-eighties, limited partnerships were all the rage. Subscribers could deduct losses calculated at many times the amount of their original investment; taxwise, therefore, having losses was almost better than making profits. In 1986, the Tax Reform Act removed most of these benefits, however, and now the investors have to pray for successful films.

A limited partnership has two kinds of partners. The General Partner, who is often called a "sponsor" or "syndicator," has unlimited liability with respect to the obligations of the partnerships and is active in management. The General Partner chooses the investments and does not have to ask for the advice or agreement of the other partners. The Limited Partners, who provide all of the capital, share any profits or losses and are not actively involved in management. In addition, their liability is limited to the amount of their investment. Gains and losses flow through directly to the Limited Partners.

With a general withdrawal of investors from the market, limited partnerships in general and film partnerships in particular have had a more difficult time. The legions of medical groups to whom entrepreneurs formerly sold the documents became disaffected and moved on. The offerings are still a valid form of financing, but you may have to find your own investors rather than rely on brokers or other agents.

A public limited partnership must be registered with the SEC, and there must be a properly prepared prospectus that includes all the facts about the partnership. The prospectus must also include a business plan (be still, my heart!) and subscription documents. Limited partnerships can remain private if they are sold within a single state.

Do not write your own limited partnership agreement. Because of the cost of attorneys, film producers are fond of writing their own documents by cutting and pasting old ones. Do not do this. When it comes to fraud, working with unofficial documents is only one aspect. Any misrepresentation about the company's plans also constitutes fraud The SEC and the Internal Revenue Service are not known for their senses of humor, and ignorance is not an acceptable defense.

Private Placements

Another form of raising funds is the private placement, also known as a Regulation D offering. The private placement is not offered to the public. It was developed to aid small businesses and is an exempt transaction, which means that the security is exempt from federal and state securities registration. Advertising is not allowed, and a notice of sale must be filed with the SEC for public partnerships. In addition, the issuer must believe that the unaccredited investor is sophisticated or is buying through a "knowledgeable purchase representative," such as an attorney or accountant. Private placements must meet disclosure requirements, and anti-fraud provisions still apply.

Advantages and Disadvantages

On the plus side, the Limited Partners have no right to interfere with the creative process. Private placements provide a means to raise funds from multiple investors without having to negotiate different deals with each one. The subscription documents contain all the deal information.

There are disadvantages as well. Because of the complicated nature of all SEC regulations and the differences between public and private offerings, participating in one of these formats requires research and expert advice from an attorney. The law is complex, and ignoring any filing regulation (each state has its own requirements) may bring an order for you to cease and desist in your sale of the offering. Another disadvantage is that the producer or the purchase representative must have a previous relationship with the investor before approaching her or him with a specific offering.

Limited Liability Companies

In the past few years, a new financial structure, the limited liability company, has become popular. LLCs are a hybrid combination of the partnership and corporate structures. They are an attractive alternative to partnerships and corporations, because the LLC provides limited personal liability to the investors, who are referred to as "members." It also provides a single level of tax. In the standard limited partnership, general partners (read "filmmakers" here) have personal liability for partnership debts, whereas limited partners have no personal liability. The worst thing that happens is that they lose their investment. In addition, the limited partners cannot participate in management without jeopardizing their limited liability status. In an LLC, members can participate in the entity's management without risking loss of limited liability. For federal tax purposes, the LLC generally is classified as a partnership. The same is true in most states— the operative word here being *most*. I have clients who have formed an LLC in Michigan, for example, but not in Florida, where the LLC is taxed as a corporation. As there is no uniformity in the LLC statutes across states, creating an LLC with members in more than one state may be complicated. It is best to contact an attorney with experience in forming this new structure. Unfortunately, in this land of ours, the way conflicts become clear is through legal decisions in courts.

At this time, the LLC as a financial vehicle is too new for a body of court cases to exist. When pass-through of revenue is of primary concern, strict conformance to IRS and state revenue accounting criteria should be considered before the LLC is chosen over the better-established partnership and "S Corporation."

BANK LOANS

Bank loans are not associated with business plans per se. However, this discussion focuses on what you will tell potential investors, and bank financing may be relevant to your situation.

Banks are in the business of renting money for a fee. They have no interest in the brilliance of your potential films; they do not care that you are a nice person and have a sparkling reputation. By law, commercial banks (the ones that give you checking accounts) can only lend money based on measurable risk, and the only credit they can take is the collateral, or the assets being offered to secure the loan. The contracts that have already been discussed—negative pickups, distribution agreements, and presales—are such collateral (assets offered to offset the bank's risk). The bank does not have to worry about when you deliver the film or how the box office performs; it is the distributor who has that worry.

The cost of the loan is tied to the prime rate, which is the rate of interest that banks pay to borrow from the Federal Reserve. It is a floating number that may fluctuate significantly. Home lending rates, also based on the prime rate, are a good example. When the prime rate falls, everyone rushes to refinance their mortgages.

In most commercial lending, loans to "low-risk" firms (for example, major studios) are 1/2 to 1 percent above the prime rate. On the other hand, a small production company, which represents a higher risk, would pay up to 3 percent above prime. Let's say that the bank is going to charge 2 percentage points above prime and that prime is 9 percent. The total would be 11 percent. On a $1-million loan, therefore, the bank removes $110,000 ($1 million multiplied by 0.11). To hedge their risk, the bank also retains another 1 or 2 percent in case the prime rate goes up. If the bank charges 1 percent, another $10,000 is added to their retained amount. Now you are down to $880,000 for the film. The bank is not through with you yet, however. It also charges you for its attorneys' fees, which can range from $15,000 for a simple contract to six figures if several companies are involved. Of course, you will still have to pay your own legal fees.

Once again we come back to the subject of attorneys. The one who represents you must know the ins and outs of all these contracts, so you should hire an experienced entertainment attorney. Costs go up drastically if your attorney is charging you an hourly rate to learn how the entertainment industry works. General corporate attorneys may mean well, but they can be an expensive choice.

Advantages and Disadvantages

The first advantage is that the producer is not personally liable for the loan; they can't take your house. A company is established for the production of the film, which is its only asset. In addition, many producers prefer to pay back a loan rather than give up equity.

On the down side, the process to obtain a loan is expensive, and several parties and miles of paperwork are involved. Also, if the distributor defaults on the loan, the bank takes possession of the film.

COMPLETION GUARANTORS

Misunderstood by neophyte filmmakers is the role of the completion guarantor. This is not the person you go to for the rest of your production money; the guarantor's role is to provide an assurance that the film will be completed and delivered to the distributor. The contract with the producer or distributor allows the guarantor to take over the film to complete it if need be.

For the bond itself, the guarantor charges a fee based on the film's budget. The charges have been flexible over the last few years, depending on the state of the completion business. The bond is not issued until after funding is in place, however, and this is often a difficult fact to explain to investors. To make matters worse, small films have trouble getting bonded anyway. The risk is too great for most guarantors to bond low-budget films. In 1993, two of the three biggest bond companies (and, according to some bankers, these three are the only acceptable firms) ran into problems. The active companies had their hands full with major productions, leaving little time or inclination to consider your $1-million film. In the last two years, new companies have come into the market, making the completion bond more accessible for smaller films.

WHAT DO YOU TELL INVESTORS?

A section on financing techniques is required as part of your business plan package. Give investors only relevant information, not everything in this chapter. Based on the assumption that your readers are not film sophisticates, you should explain what constitutes a presale agreement, a negative pickup, or whatever form of financing you will pursue. Be prepared to answer investors' questions. They may ask you about the forms of financing that you have not included. You should be conversant enough with the pros and cons of various strategies to explain your choices intelligently.

As mentioned earlier, it is unproductive to include financing methods that you do not plan to use. If you plan to use a limited partnership, for example, the business plan will be part of the offering; otherwise, there is no reason to discuss this form of financing. To do so would be to create a red herring for investors, confusing them with a nonexistent choice. Along the same lines, you should be careful about considering options that may no longer exist. What Canada or Australia does in 1997 may not be relevant in 1998 or 1999. Financing patterns, like everything else in our culture, can be in or out of vogue from year to year. It is important to keep current with the business climate through the trades and other sources while writing your plan.

8

The Financial Plan

Get your facts first, then you can distort them as you please.

MARK TWAIN

FORECASTING WITHOUT FEAR

Predicting the future has been popular since the days of Nostradamus. No one can afford to run a business without looking ahead. Only when you have a clear picture of your company's potential growth can you proceed with a feeling of confidence. In the past 500 years, little has changed except the technology. For filmmakers, predicting the revenue of films yet to be made is a necessity. This chapter reviews how to find data, what to do with it after you find it, and how to create your own financial forecasts.

Every time I assign students the task of looking up box office grosses, they object. Their idea of a business plan is a description of their films and, possibly, general market and distribution information. Although important, these items pale in importance to projected income. Remember the investors? They are going to read the Executive Summary first and then go quickly to the revenues and expenses. Money is the concrete that holds these building blocks together. Before investors hand over hard cash, they want to believe that your project will be profitable. Forecasting is an art, albeit not a precise one. Sophisticated business writers like to say that the one sure thing about a prediction is that it will be wrong; they are probably right. The value of a forecast is as a guide for making decisions; the better informed the forecaster, the closer to actual events the forecast will be. By researching history, looking for relationships among the data you find, and making assumptions about the future based on those relationships, you have a basis for predicting your future grosses.

Anyone Can Do It

There is no mystery to forecasting revenues and expenses. You do not have to be an accountant or hold an MBA. You do not need a previous knowledge of trend analysis, regression and correlation points, or internal rate of return. This jargon is used by financial whiz kids to speak to one another; life can go on without it.

The information that you uncover can be used to create the numbers that make a company look feasible. You will take the elements that seem to influence the outcome of a film—genre, stars, director, distribution, ancillary returns—and analyze how much you think each will influence the resulting revenue. The only math skills you will need are adding, subtracting, multiplying, and dividing. Mix these skills with a little gut feeling, and you have a forecast. If you can balance your checkbook, you can create a forecast.

FINDING THE DATA

In predicting the future revenues for your films (or other projects), you need to know what has happened in the recent (that is, not 1975) past. Where do you look? You might try trade papers, industry magazines, regular newspapers and magazines, festivals and film markets, seminars, and other industry meetings. These sources were discussed in Chapter 5.

Let's look at some specific data that you can uncover in your research. Every Tuesday, the trade papers (*The Hollywood Reporter* and *Daily Variety*) publish the 60 top-grossing films for the previous weekend. The box office grosses in these tables equal the total domestic gross sales for the film. Since they include Canada, the grosses are really North American, but for convenience we will refer to them as U.S. grosses. The majority of the films on the list used to be studio productions. However, for the last few years, 28–35 of those films in any given week are independent. In addition, *Weekly Variety* (published on Sundays) has the accumulated foreign box-office totals for the films. In a separate table, it shows the ten top-grossing films in each of 10 foreign markets. (Note: The number of countries they list changes from time to time.) *The Hollywood Reporter* has a similar table of foreign totals on Tuesday.

Now you have a beginning. Let us say that you want to know the box office totals, number of screens, etc., for *Shine*, and it is April 8, 1997. Looking in *Daily Variety*, the U.S. box office gross (remember, this includes the exhibitor) is $34.7 million. The film is on 719 screens and has been in release for 136 days, or a little over 19 weeks. If you want to follow the revenue from the beginning, you can look up all the weekly issues back to November 28, 1996. Its first appearance on the list shows a box office of $162,179 from seven screens after three days in release. You can also track how long it took the film to reach a particular number of screens (911 is the highest number, but the film is still in release), and you can determine the average gross per screen for each weekend.

The box office grosses are collected and estimated by a company called Entertainment Data, Inc. (EDI). Because the weekly lists contain no more than 60 films, a film might continue in release but not have a high enough box office to appear on the charts for its entire theatrical run. Experience shows that the trade lists give a majority of the grosses. Occasionally, a film will reappear on the list as it begins to rise in total box office again. *Fargo* finished its initial domestic release, or at least left the weekly charts, in September 1996 with a total gross of $24.1 million. It reappeared in March 1997, following the Oscar nominations, and to date has grossed $24.5 million. Lists published annually give a total recap of many of the film grosses, but you may not have the time to wait that long. If you do not subscribe to one of these papers and your local college library does not have them, check the major booksellers. Many of them carry *Weekly Variety* and sometimes the daily trades. The foreign box-office figures are more perplexing, as a film may be released in different territories over a two-year period after its domestic release.

Many films are too small to appear on the trade paper lists; these are harder to track. I keep my own database, but also look to other services for hard-to-find data. In addition, if you read at least one of the trades every day, you will see reports on the grosses for some smaller films in individual theaters. They do not cover every town and theater in America, however.

I also encourage clients and students to call the producers of the film in which they are interested. Independent filmmakers are very generous with one other. Having someone interested enough in your film to call is very flattering. Alternatively, you might call the distributor, if it is a smallish company. When *The Living End* fell off the trade charts at $700,000, I called Jon Gerrans and Marcus Hu at Strand Releasing, the original distributor, and learned the film actually grossed close to $1 million. For this edition, I checked with them about *Stonewall*, one of my favorites from last year. Instead of the reported $630,000, it also grossed just under $1 million. Distributors love to report high grosses.

Budgets are another story. Depending on whether the filmmaker is looking for a distributor or wants to brag about how well the grosses have done on a low budget, you may or may not know the real budget. Unfortunately, the revenue is only part of the story. A $24.5 million gross with a budget of $6.5 million is a lot more impressive than it would be with a budget of $10 million. You have to go with the best information you can get. Try not to make them up. There are enough resources out there to find a reference to the budget. If you are really into keeping your own database, the U.K. trade paper *Screen International* is another good resource.

Again, interviews with filmmakers in the public press are a good source. Check the week or two before release. For recent film releases, check television and radio shows for the appearance of a filmmaker. Even before the 1997 Oscar nominations, young filmmakers were appearing more often on the morning and evening talk shows than they had before. Watch CNN, E! Entertainment Channel, Oprah, Charlie Rose, and all the news programs, especially on the all-news channels. In recent years, the Independent Film Channel and the Sundance Channel have gone on the air in selected markets; naturally, they are dedicated to information about independent films.

The film festivals are another place to gather extensive financial information. Many producers and directors of independent films attend, and they will usually answer questions about not only the cost of their films, but also the source of their financing. People often feel more comfortable about revealing proprietary data face-to-face. Also watch the Oscar telecast and the Cannes Film Festival Awards (broadcast on Bravo). You never know what you might learn.

What about older movies? For this book, my assistant, Faryl, researched the grosses and budgets for films that were released before 1990 for Table 5.1. *Off Hollywood* by David Rosen and *Making Movies* by John Russo contained some of the data we needed. Then she went to the library and checked the periodical indices under the names of the directors and the films to locate relevant interviews and articles. In addition, she checked the trade papers for the year of release of each film. We were able to obtain enough articles and figures from *The New York Times, Newsweek,* and *Variety* to complete the table.

Now that you have the box-office and budget figures, you can estimate the rentals (review the tables in Chapter 4). It has been assumed that 50 percent is the studio's average share of the box office and that 47 percent (up from 45 percent in the early to mid-90s) is the amount returned to the independent distributor. In working with these numbers, it is necessary to use the average return. If you are projecting your own film with a specific distribution or booking method, then you can figure that into your equation.

Foreign and Other Data

Foreign rentals are harder to obtain. The handiest published sources are the international charts in *Weekly Variety* and *The Hollywood Reporter.* The former covers more countries. Because these papers cover only the top 10 films in each country, very few independent films can be tracked this way. However, for many independent films, such as *Set It Off* and *Lone Star,* these lists can be a good source.

It might take two years to know the total foreign results of an American film. Release dates are staggered around the globe. The "windows" of release can be used for estimating the timing of foreign returns. For your purposes, using the total return is acceptable. You can also use Table 8.1 to get an estimate on each country. Keep it to yourself, however, and only give your investors total foreign numbers. If anyone expects you to estimate each country separately, resist the urge. You may be painting yourself into a corner; remember what we said about implied promises?

The vast majority of foreign theatrical revenues arrive within 15 to 24 months of the U.S. release. If you are doing a business plan in February of 1998, therefore, worldwide data may only be available for films released in early to mid-1996; U.S. gross data is up-to-the-minute, of course.

Revenues from cable, free television, video, and other ancillary sources are published in the individual industry trade journals and newsletters. To find the results for specific films, you may end up having to spend money on a consulting firm, such as Business Strategies. Magazines published specifically for the video and cable industries are also a good source of data. Check local libraries, especially at the film schools, to see what information they carry.

Occasionally, U.S. and worldwide numbers are reported in articles that sum up the past year. You may also be able to find models, such as the one in Table 4.2. Models are not meant to represent any particular film but give you a measure of the average. They are published in books and occasionally trade papers.

Average Foreign Revenues

Several sources provide the latest information on typical revenues from individual foreign territories. *The Hollywood Reporter, Variety,* and *Screen International* present tables once a year, usually during AFM. The films are divided into budget categories, such as $1 to $5 million or $5 to $10 million. The classifications depend on who has provided the list. They provide high and low prices for theatrical films.

The American Film Marketing Association releases a table of global sales every year that is reprinted in several industry papers and magazines. In addition, some of the foreign trade magazines gather data. Usually, these numbers are released around the time of the American Film Market and can be obtained there quite easily. You might also research the trade papers for late February and early March, when the market is held.

Table 8.1, "Potential Sales by Territory for Budgets up to $2 Million" is a compilation of average territory sales gathered from individual distributors. These numbers are not box office totals, but represent the average advances from distributors in that territory. As this may be the only money you ever get from them, you can use it to get a general idea of your prospects. The range of likely prices is based on the distributors' experience selling low-budget films. When forecasting, you always want to be conservative, so you would use the average return of dollars. For example, looking at Japan, you see the high is $200,000 and the low is $50,000. This does not mean that all distributors will pay you $200,000; generally, the most they will pay is 10 percent of the budget. Use the average figure, which is $125,000.

What Has Happened?

There is no question about it: You must analyze this data before putting it into your proposal. I have said it before, but filmmakers

Table 8.1 Potential Sales by Territory for Budgets up to $2 Million ($ thousands)

Country	High	Low	Average
Asia			
Japan	200	50	125
Indonesia	50	25	38
Korea	100	34	67
Hong Kong	30	10	20
India	25	15	20
Taiwan	35	10	23
Philippines	35	10	23
Other	100	50	75
Total Asia	575	204	390*
Australia	75	35	55
Europe			
Great Britain	150	60	105
Germany	200	60	130
France	160	50	105
Italy	100	45	73
Scandinavia	140	35	88
Spain	100	25	63
Holland	45	15	30
Other	100	45	73
Total Europe	995	335	665*
South America			
Mexico	60	15	38
Other	50	30	40
Total South America	110	45	78*
Middle East	25	5	15

Note: Sales dollars courtesy of various distributors.
*Do not total the averages.

have convinced me that I cannot say it too often. This analysis is your job, not the investor's. Do not expect the investor to accidentally happen upon useful information while browsing through the 15 or 20 pages you have photocopied from newspapers and magazines. It is your duty to find useful information and present it in an easily under-standable way.

The data that you gather about previously released films will serve two purposes: (1) show the profits (if any) of films recently released, and (2) supply a basis for estimating the revenues for your films. The first part of your numerical story consists of showing what has happened with films that have already been produced and released. You use these examples to build a case for the ultimate success of your film. Select recent films that have a relation to your planned production in terms of genre, budget, or other common factors. Try not to go back more than three years, as changes in box office make older films less comparable. If you are dealing with a new or recent genre, of course, you may not have this option.

Genre is a common way to group films; however, use whatever characteristic you feel links these films together. When the business plan for lesbian-themed films, described earlier, was being written in 1992, few successful films in that genre had been released. The first two films in the company's plan were under $3 million, and for these, we tracked the available films with gay themes. The third film was projected to have a $10- to $15-million budget. No similar films existed in that budget range, so we created an additional table of 16 recently released films with budgets up to $15 million. The table showed gross receipts, negative costs, prints and ads, and domestic gross profit in order to give as current a picture as possible.

Whatever your rationale for grouping films, use budget clusters that make sense. Grouping films in the $5- to $10-million range, for example, would be better than grouping films in the $100,000 to $10-million range. The ultimate results would be varied for a number of reasons, including production values, cost of prints and ads, and quality of cast. On the other hand, too small a budget range, such as $100,000 to $300,000, might include several films, but how many would be similar in story or theme?

The films you include in your business plan depend on what is available. It is better to pick films that appear to have at least broken even. If you must include films that have lost money, be prepared to explain why your film will succeed where others have failed. Another warning: DO NOT INVENT NUMBERS. If lying does not bother you, getting caught in a lie will. Then the game will be over. If box office grosses are all you can find, then that is what you must use.

Tables A.1 through A.3, A.5, and A.6, included with the sample Business Plan in the appendix, are examples of methods for presenting this information. Tables A.1 and A.2 are based on films of the same genre; Table A.3 is based on budget groupings. Tables A.5 and A.6 show the projected revenues and their flow over time. (For purposes of illustration, these films are fictional.) These sample tables include seven items:

1. *Domestic theatrical rentals:* Domestic rentals are the portion of the U.S. theatrical box-office that reverts back to the distributor (or producer). (The tables in the trades commonly include Canadian box-office figures in this total.) If only box-office figures are available, you can assume 47 percent of the total for this number. For individual films, it could be a little lower or higher.

   When working with numbers, you should avoid factoring in exceptional movies that would make all your averages too high, such as *Four Weddings and a Funeral*. With a negative cost of $4.5 million, the film earned $52.7 million in the U.S. and $100 million worldwide. List it and indicate in a footnote that it is in your chart for reference only. Just as on any given day any team can win, it is theoretically possible for any film to be a breakout hit. For purposes of estimating and projecting, however, you should use more common results. Mark Twain said, "There are three kinds of lies: lies, damned lies and statistics." Reflect on this.

2. *Domestic ancillary revenue:* The ancillary revenue includes all nontheatrical sources, such as cable, video, free television, syndicated television, and pay-per-view. Previously, video was a major source of revenue, and advances were routinely sought. In the last few years, however, the picture has changed. Video is not as big a business anymore. Pay-per-view (movies on demand) is growing, although not as quickly as the companies expected three years ago. The windows for cable have changed and the premium channels are getting movies sooner than they used to. Unless you have a deal in the works, do not plan on advances from cable. HBO and Showtime advance money on films being made for their own use. A few of the for-cable films have had a U.S. theatrical

release, but only after they have played on cable. In the past, PBS has also financed films that have had a subsequent theatrical release. There is no indication, however, that this strategy is a general policy.

3. *Foreign theatrical revenue:* The distributor is responsible for collecting money from the foreign box office, which includes all countries except the U.S. and Canada. All monies counted as foreign revenue in your tables can be added to the domestic rentals figure, as the exhibitors' portion already has been removed. Always be sure that you are comparing apples to apples.

   Some films that do only moderately well in the United States do much better overseas, although generally the U.S. theatrical results drive the foreign box office. If a picture does not perform well in U.S. theaters, it normally makes all other theatrical and ancillary venues worth less money. The type of film and the stars often have a lot to do with these results. However, a genre or actor may make a difference. Certain U.S. television stars continually appear in movies of the week, for instance, because they have large followings in foreign markets. This fact does not mean that distributors will accept them in your feature films. There are other films that do well in domestic and foreign video but have weak box offices.

4. *Foreign ancillary revenue:* Foreign ancillary presents great opportunity. Television companies often buy exclusive product. In addition, markets have opened up in Eastern Europe and Asia. Distributors report that Southeast Asia and India are becoming much stronger. The potential revenues for English-language films, even small ones, in other countries remain much stronger than for foreign-language films in the United States.

5. *Total revenue:* This is self-explanatory.

6. *Negative cost, prints and ads, and total costs:* We have already discussed finding the production, or negative, costs of the film. These are not the total costs, however. Prints and ads are an important expense. It is necessary to include these costs to get a total profit picture. As films stay in distribution, the P&A costs grow. Therefore, if you are forecasting the initial release cost, indicate it.

7. *Gross profit (loss):* Gross profit (loss) equals the revenue minus the direct expenses before the company operating expenses. In

this case, direct expenses are the negative and prints and ads costs. They relate directly to your film, as compared to the company overhead costs, which exist whether a film is in production or not. Notice the parentheses around the word *loss*. When preparing financial statements, use parentheses rather than minus signs to indicate negative numbers. Both words can be written on the profit line. I would recommend forecasting a profit; otherwise, you may want to rethink the whole idea.

WHAT TO DO WITH THOSE PESKY NUMBERS

Now we come to your films, represented in Tables A.1 through A.3. Here are two guidelines for projecting your revenues. First, be conservative. The rule of thumb is to forecast your income on the low end and your expenses on the high end. Probably all filmmakers who have ever done a budget have padded it to be sure that they did not run out of money. You want to take the opposite path for revenues. If you are making a $3-million black-themed film from the viewpoint of the "bad kids," you may be overly optimistic to assume that the film will gross close to $30 million, as *Menace II Society* did. For one thing, that film was at the Director's Fortnight at Cannes. It is nice to aspire to being accepted at such a prestigious festival, but you can't plan on it. Bring your average revenues down at least $10 million to be on the safe side.

Second, be honest. As long as the data of your historical films are as accurate as possible and the films you choose are comparable to those you plan to make, you should be all right. The comment made to me most often by distributors and investors is, "Tell them not to include *The Crying Game* or *Four Weddings and a Funeral* as average films." Feel free to discuss them in your analysis as an example of an exceptional result to hold out the brass ring as a hook for the investor. As long as you use those terms, you will be okay.

Assumptions

Before seizing your calculator, you should write down your assumptions. Unless you have concrete reasons for the forecasted revenues in your tables, people may assume that you invented them. There has to be a thought process leading to these numbers. If you have just written 15 or 20 pages for the preceding sections, you have already gone through the thought process. In most cases, the crucial elements have already been mentioned, and the list is a recap for your benefit and for the investor's. Do not expect readers to remember the specifics from the body of the business plan; this is not a game of hide and seek with the investor.

Explain your assumptions at the end of your Financial Section directly before the tables to be sure that the reader knows how you came to your conclusions. If you do not do this, it may look like you have no rationale. Review the assumptions in the sample business plan before continuing.

Risk Factors

Every business plan requires a statement of risk in which you tell investors what a high-risk investment it is. Make it clear that nothing is guaranteed. No entrepreneur likes a risk statement, but it is a protection for you. In a limited partnership prospectus, your attorney will insert one whether you like it or not. You are well advised to do this in any proposal for funds. With a risk statement included in your business plan, investors cannot later claim that they did not know the investment was unpredictable. Even though it seems obvious to you, and probably to them, assume nothing and state the facts anyway.

It can be a very short statement or a long explanation. In the business plan for one limited partnership, the risk statement runs 14 pages, but this is a bit excessive. Where should you include the risk statement? I normally create a separate section. As space is at a premium here, it is included with the assumptions. If you are at a loss for words, please borrow the one in the book or from the prospectus of one or two companies that have gone public. And please do not add sentences such as, "Our proposal has no risk, because it is sure to win an Academy Award." You can put that anywhere else, except among the risk declarations.

Revenue and Cash Flow

Table A.5 shows the projected income for a fictional company that is planning to produce three films over a five-year period. This projection is based on the results of movies made between 1992 and 1995. By the time you do your plan, a $500,000 film might be doing better or worse at the box office. Looking at the numbers, you can take the average of all the films or the median (the point above and below which half the films fall), or you can give more weight to the more recent films. It depends on whether you feel that the genre is gaining more audience approval or has been drawing the same amount of box office dollars for the past few years. You have to look at the available data and use good judgment.

A cash flow statement shows the timing of incoming revenue and outgoing cash. The dollars will not come in all in one week or one month. Table A.6 shows a sample cash flow statement. Notice that in the columns for the table, I have used Year 1, Year 2, Year 3, and so on. If you are looking for the production money, your year starts when that money is in the bank. To specify the first year—for example, 1998—could create a problem. What if you are still wandering around two years later looking for money? Finding money is hard; no need to announce it to your current prospect. In addition, each year is further divided into quarters. This seems to make the most sense for showing cash flow. However, you can use whole years. I would shy away from individual months. The format is hard to read and includes more detail than is necessary. Unless you have the distributor's monthly accounts for various films in front of you, there is no way to track such data accurately.

In the sample cash flow statement, all of the production money is outgoing in Year 1. I have assumed one year from the beginning to the end of post-production. If you are an experienced filmmaker, you may be able to shorten this time frame. Release of the film is scheduled for six months after the end of post-production. No one really knows, even if you already have distribution guaranteed. But we are using estimates, promising a specific interval. The first rentals are shown during the quarter in which distribution begins. Film revenues normally start slowly in the first quarter, build in the second, and then taper down over three more quarters. One reason to track domestic grosses week to week is to find trends in the number of theaters and the amount of grosses. Going through that exercise will reveal a pattern that you can use.

Average release "windows" (the period that has to pass after the theatrical release before the film may be released in the ancillary markets) give you an idea of the money flow from other sources. Again, not all films are released the same ways. Some countries actually legislate the time period; in other cases, the distributor negotiates it. Trying to figure this out country by country would be excessive. The timing has been very fluid lately, so it is a good idea to research the topic to keep current.

In the sample statement, the film goes into foreign release in the third quarter of Year 2, approximately seven months after the domestic release date. All the foreign revenues have been grouped into one category. The film goes into domestic ancillary markets at the same time. The current release pattern is still video and pay-per-view, followed by other cable channels. Keep your eye on the news, however; changes are in the wind.

The total line is the sum of the incoming cash minus the outgoing cash. Because the production costs for the second film begin in the second year, production and prints and ads expenses appear as a deduction from the incoming cash flow. In a multi-picture company, the cash flow statement allows you to see whether you will have enough money coming in to keep production going. Do not panic over minus totals. The timing of eventual profit is the deciding factor.

The cumulative total is simply the sum of the totals from quarter to quarter, showing the position in profit and loss. These numbers represent the profits and losses from the films only. To keep the table simple for our purposes, the company overhead numbers have not been included; however, you need to include them for the overall company picture. In real life, ongoing costs that cannot be assigned to a specific picture must be included to show the company's total cash position at any point in time.

RUNNING THE COMPANY

An ongoing company has its past history to report, along with a statement of its present position. Your accountant will do the serious reports for you, such as Sources and Uses of Funds, Balance Sheet, and so on. These go into your Financial Planning section along with the other tables.

New companies have less to report. There may or may not be a bank account worth mentioning. Sample Tables A.4 (Administrative Expenses) and A.5 (Estimated Income Statement) present information that must be included in the business plan, even for a very small company.

Administrative (Overhead) Expenses

If you are setting up a company, you will have ongoing expenses, no matter what films you are making. These are the overhead expenses discussed in Chapter 4. Your company's overhead will be far less than that of the studios, of course. These general administrative costs include salaries that are not attributable to a specific film budget as well as all of the company's tools of the trade—office equipment, telephone charges, entertainment costs, and so on.

Table A.4 provides an example of items that might be included as administrative expenses. Your company may have fewer people or no salaried employees at all. Before Year 1, there are generally startup expenses. You may rent an office, option a script, buy a computer, take a trip to the Dardanelles. Any expenses that are necessary to get your company going are shown in this table. Even if you wait for investment funds before doing any startup, list these costs separately. Some of them—like the computer—are one-time costs.

Like everything else, administrative costs are projected over the time period of the business plan. Look ahead to the number of films that you plan to make three or four years down the road. You may need additional office staff, more office space, or increased development money. Everyone knows that these numbers are guesstimates; however, as a general rule, you should include all the expenses you can think of. On the other hand, do not give yourself a salary of $1 million. I see this item in a lot of companies that never get funded. Because you are partners with the investor, your salary should be moderate.

Income Statement

The Estimated Income Statement (Table A.5), also known as the "Statement of Revenues and Expenses," is the profit statement for the company as a whole. The sample shows a simple production company in which all the income is from films. If you are planning to produce other products, such as video, you will need several revenue lines to show each product separately. You should also provide separate assumptions and cash flows for those products because they function differently from film. Then make a combined statement that includes all the products.

The net profit (loss) line is the sum of the company's revenues and expenses. Commonly, the phrase "before taxes" is added to indicate that this is a preliminary income forecast. Do not let these phrases throw you. An accountant can easily prepare these statements for you.

After you have reviewed Chapter 1, "Executive Summary," study the sample business plan that follows this chapter. It was written for a fictional company. Feel free to use this format as a guide for developing your own business plan. Certain factual items in the text may be out of date by the time you read this book. What is important for you, however, is not the specifics, but the methodology. Have fun, and good luck!

_____ Appendix

Sample Business Plan for a Fictional Company

CRAZED CONSULTANT FILMS INTERNATIONAL

FOR INFORMATION ONLY

This memorandum is a business plan. It is not an offering for sale of any securities of the company. It is for your confidential use only and may not be reproduced, sold, or redistributed without the prior approval of Crazed Consultant Films International (CCFI).

EXECUTIVE SUMMARY

Overview

Crazed Consultant Films International is a start-up enterprise engaged in the development and production of motion picture films for theatrical release. CCFI's goals are to make films that will raise the consciousness of the American public about the importance of household cats and that will be commercially exploitable to a mass audience. The company plans to produce three films over the next five years, with budgets ranging from $500,000 to $10 million.

Management Team

At the core of CCFI are the founders, who bring to the company successful entrepreneurial experience and in-depth expertise in motion

155

picture production. The team is complemented by a support group of consultants and advisers.

The Product

CCFI owns options on Jane Lovable's first three *Leonard the Wonder Cat* books and has first refusal on the next three publications. Currently, one book is in print, another is about to be published, and a third is still in the writing stage. The first book has created an established audience for the films.

The movies, based on Lovable's series, will star Leonard, a half-Siamese, half-mongrel cat, whose adventures make for entertaining stories that incorporate a strong moral lesson. CCFI expects each film to stand on its own and to produce profits to finance each successive film. The movies are designed to capture the interest of the entire family, building significantly on an already established base.

The Industry

The total gross box office receipts for 1996 were $5.9 billion as reported by the MPAA. This figure represents admissions of $1.3 billion based on National Association of Theater Owners (NATO) average ticket prices. In the past five years, box office receipts have increased 23.1 percent, and the number of ticket buyers has increased 17.4 percent. Despite many ups and downs, such as the advent of television and the growth of the home video market, theatrical distribution has continued to prosper. Theatrical rentals are forecasted to be $3.5 billion in the U.S. and $7.5 billion worldwide in the year 2001.

The structure of the motion picture business has been changing over the past few years. And while U.S. theatrical distribution is still the first choice of any feature-length film, international markets are gaining even greater strength than they had before. Independent films have been steadily gaining market share in the 1990s. Today the worldwide market for these films is estimated to be $3 billion.

The Market

Family films with sophisticated and updated story lines have been making a comeback at the box office. The public is ready for mainstream films that present feline themes. The commercial success in recent years of animal films, such as *Babe*, have opened the door for the cat. As the pet owned by more individuals than any other animal, the cat will draw audiences from far and wide.

It has historically been true that in hard economic times, family entertainment wins out. People want to be entertained and forget their troubles. We feel that films that offer diversion and feature a strong cat story line will draw a large audience.

Heretofore, the majority of family films have been by studios. We believe that the time is right to make cost-effective films on smaller budgets. Once the cat genre has become popular, our films will be able to move into large commercial theaters. Crazed Consultant Films International plans to keep its films independent in order to maintain quality of story and filming.

Distribution

The Company will seek distribution by independent companies whose proven ability to handle low-budget films with sensitive themes appeals to CCFI's desire for special handling. We will hold screenings specifically for the distributors in Los Angeles and/or New York. We will contact individually some of the distributors who have experience with the family film genre. In addition, we will take the films to markets and film festivals where appropriate.

The foreign markets have become more profitable for family films in the past few years. As our reputation for quality films grows, both domestic and foreign markets will be anxious to buy our product. CCFI expects to have- increasing leverage over the next few years in negotiating deals and attracting major cast and directoral elements.

Investment Opportunity and Financial Highlights

The founders are seeking an equity investment of approximately $20 million for production of three films and overhead expenditures. Current projections indicate a pretax net profit of $29.2 million, a 46 percent profit on the initial investment for all three films. CCFI will also entertain proposals to make one film at a time and roll those profits over into the subsequent films.

THE COMPANY

Crazed Consultant Films International is a privately owned California corporation that was established in September 1996. Our principal purpose and business is to create theatrical motion pictures. The Company plans to develop and produce quality family-themed films portraying positive images of the household cat.

The public is ready for films with feline themes. Big budget animal-themed films have opened the market over the last five years. In addition, the changing balance of cat over dog owners is an allegory for changes in society overall. The objectives of CCFI are as follows:

1. To produce quality films that provide positive family entertainment with moral tales designed for both enjoyment and education.
2. To make films that will celebrate the importance of the household cat and that will be exploitable to a mass audience.
3. To produce three feature films in the first five years, with budgets ranging from $500,000 to $10 million.
4. To develop scripts with outside writers.
5. To explore overseas co-production and co-financing potential for the company.
6. To distribute our films through independent distribution companies.
7. To negotiate distribution agreements on a film-by-film basis.

There is a need and a hunger for more family films. We believe that we can make exciting films starting as low as $500,000 without sacrificing quality. Until recently, there was a dearth of cat films. Far more attention has been paid to dogs, who are alleged to be "man's best friend." However, the emergence of cats as the most popular pet in the United States has changed that picture. Cats are at least woman's best friend, and women often drive the box office.

We plan to change movie emphasis from pigs and dogs to cats, while providing meaningful and wholesome entertainment that will attract the entire family. In view of the growth of the family market in the last few years, the cat theme is one that has been undervalued and, consequently, underexploited. Part of the growth has been due to the historical success of "feel-good" films during economic downturns; in addition, there has been a general worldwide emphasis on returning to traditional family values. For these reasons, animal films with sophisticated and modern story lines have been making a comeback at the box office and appeal to moviegoers of all ages.

CCFI's films will feature Leonard, hero of Jane Lovable's *Leonard the Wonder Cat* books. The Company perceives a large, presold audience. The first book in the series has sold 10 million copies not only to children and preteens but teenagers and adults as well.

Management and Organization

The primary strength of any company is in its management team. CCFI's principals, Ms. Lotta Mogul and Mr. Gimme Bucks, have extensive experience in business and in the entertainment industry. In addition, the company has relationships with key consultants and advisers who will be available to fill important roles on an as-needed basis. The following individuals make up the current management team and key managers:

Ms. Lotta Mogul, President and Executive Producer

Ms. Mogul spent three years at Jeffcarl Studios as a producer. Among her many credits are *Walter of Wisconsin, The Dog Came for Dinner*, and *Fluffy and Fido Go to College*. These films all had budgets under $10 million and had combined grosses of more than $300 million worldwide. As President and Executive Producer, her considerable experience will be used to create our production slate, manage the CCFI team, negotiate with distributors, and plan future strategies.

Mr. Gimme Bucks, Vice President, Financial Affairs

Mr. Bucks will oversee the long-term strategy and financial affairs of the company. A graduate of the University of California at Los Angeles, Mr. Bucks has an MBA. He worked in business affairs at XYZ Studios and has been a consultant to small, independent film companies.

Mr. Better Focus, Cinematographer

Mr. Focus is a member of the American Society of Cinematographers. He was Alpha Numerical's director of photography for several years. He won an Emmy Award for his work on *Unusual Birds of Ottumwa*, and he has been nominated twice for Academy Awards.

Ms. Ladder Climber, Production and Development

Ms. Climber will assist in the production of our films. She began her career as an assistant to the producer for the cult film *Dogs That Bark* and has worked her way up to production manager and line producer on several films. Most recently, she served as line producer on *The Paw* and *Thirty Miles to Azusa*.

We plan to hire producers for individual projects as required by the production schedule. The office staff will be lean but will expand as the work load demands. In the meantime, we are also working with the following consultants:

> **Samuel Torts**, Attorney-At-Law, Los Angeles, CA
> **Winners and Losers**, Certified Public Accountants, Los Angeles, CA

FILM PROJECTS

CCFI currently controls the rights to the first three *Leonard the Wonder Cat* books, which will be the basis for its film projects over the next five years. In March 1997, the company paid $5,000 for three-year options on the first three books with first refusal on the next three. The author will receive additional payments over the next four years as production begins. The *Leonard* series, written by Jane Lovable, has been obtained at very inexpensive option prices due to Ms. Mogul's attachment to cats. Three film projects are scheduled.

Thursday's Cat

The first film will be based on the novel *Thursday's Cat*, which has sold 10 million copies. The story revolves around the love between a girl, Natasha, and her cat, Leonard. The two leave the big city to live in a small town, where they discover the true meaning of life.

Mr. Furry Catman has written the screenplay. The projected budget for *Thursday's Cat* is $500,000, with CCFI producing and Ms. Ultra Virtuoso directing. Ms. Virtuoso's previous credits include a low-budget feature, *My Life as a Ferret*, and two rock videos, *Country Love* and *Hot Fluffy Rag*. We are currently in the development stage with this project. The initial script has been written, but we have no commitments from actors. Casting will commence once financing is in place.

As a marketing plus, the upcoming movie will be advertised on the cover of the new paperback edition of the book.

The Nine Lives of Leonard

This film is based on the second *Leonard* book, which is currently in the prepublication stage. In the story, Leonard stows away on a sailboat for adventure. He and the skipper, Henry Desire, are ship-wrecked on the mysterious island of Catalina, where they elude wild buffalo herds and weather wild rainstorms. They eventually hail a passing frigate. Leonard is reunited with his friend Natasha, and romance blossoms between Natasha and Henry.

Ms. Ultra Virtuoso is set to direct this feature also. Development on this project will start after we are in production on *Thursday's Cat*. Current estimates place the budget at $2.5 million. We plan to interview screenwriters as soon as the shooting script for the first film is finalized.

Leonard in Space

The third book in the series is currently being written by Ms. Lovable and will be published in late 1998. The story features Leonard joining the space program as its first feline crew member. Because of special effects, we estimate the cost of this film to be $10 million. Blast-off Studios will create the effects for us for partial payment up front and the rest on the back end. No director or casting has been sought for the film to date.

INDUSTRY OVERVIEW

The motion picture industry is a constantly changing and multi-faceted business. It consists of two principal activities: production and distribution. Production involves the development, financing, and making of motion pictures; distribution involves the advertising, pub-licizing, licensing, promotion and physical reproduction, delivery, and exhibition of completed motion pictures. The following is a sim-plified overview of a complex process for the purpose of describing how the business works.

Motion Picture Production

The total gross box office receipts for 1996 were $5.9 billion as reported by the MPAA. This figure represents admissions of 1.3 billion based on National Association of Theater Owners (NATO) average ticket prices. In the past five years, box office receipts have increased 23.1 percent, and the number of ticket buyers has increased 17.4 percent. Despite many ups and downs, such as the advent of television and the growth of the home video market, theatrical distribution has continued to prosper. Theatrical rentals are forecasted to be $3.5 billion in the U.S. and $7.5 billion worldwide in the year 2001.

The structure of the motion picture business has been changing over the past few years. While U.S. theatrical distribution is still the first choice of any feature-length film, international markets are gaining even greater strength than they had before. Independent films have been steadily gaining market share in the 1990s. Today the worldwide market for these films is estimated to be $3 billion.

Until recent years, the major studios all maintained extensive production facilities. With significant overhead expenses and the rise of the unions and guilds, film budgets began to rise. Studios released fewer pictures but expected greater grosses per film. As a consequence, smaller production entities, the independents, arose. Films typically are defined by the source of their financing; even though some of these production entities are public companies, much of their production financing comes through the studio system.

At a studio, a film begins in one of two ways. Someone inside the company might develop a "concept" (one or two lines of an idea), or a known writer might make the well-known "30-second pitch" and secure a deal. On the other hand, an agent might bring the script by a new writer to the attention of the studio. Scriptwriters are hired, cast sought, and directors and producers assigned. Then the film is put into development.

Development begins when the studio options or purchases a literary property, usually a script or a book. The nature of the deal depends on those involved in it. During development, the studio hires writers to adapt the book into a screenplay, reworks the original, determines a budget, and even starts casting.

The next step is preproduction, the period before principal photography when commitments are sought for talent, the director and crew are hired, and contracts are finalized and signed. Producers try to have all contracts in place before filming begins. The filming of a motion picture is called principal photography. It takes from 8 to 12 weeks, although major cast members may not be used for the entire period. Once the production has gotten to this stage, it is unlikely that a studio will shut it down. Even if the picture goes over the budget, the studio will usually find a way to complete it.

During the post-production period that follows principal photography, the film is edited and synchronized with music and dialogue. In certain cases, special effects are added. The post-production period used to require six to nine months. With recent technological developments, however, this time has been cut drastically for some films.

Theatrical Exhibition

The exhibitor pays a percentage of the picture's box office receipts (called "rentals") to the studio or distributor. The size of the percentage depends on the distributor's strength and the exhibitor's desire to show the film. A major studio release usually has a 50/50 split, while independent films average 47 percent (up from 45 percent in 1994) from the box office. Of course, the exhibitor keeps all the money for popcorn, candy, and soft drinks.

The U.S. release of a film usually ends within the first year. Major studio films may go out to as many as 3,000 screens in the first few weeks. Independent films start slower and build on their success. Although the amount of rentals will decline toward the end of the film's run, it may very well increase in the first few months. It is not unusual for a smaller film to gain theaters as it becomes more popular.

Because revenues from all other sources are driven by the success of the theatrical distribution, a film's stay on theater screens is important. Coupled with this is the exhibitor's basic desire to see people sitting in theater seats. Although the studio has some power to keep a mediocre film on the screen with its greater resources for marketing and promotion, good independent films will be shown. Exhibitors have always maintained that they will show any film they think their customers will pay to see. Depending on the location of the individual theater or the chain, local pressures may play a part in deciding which films are shown. Not all pictures are appropriate for all theaters.

Despite the new technologies on the horizon, theatrical exhibition is not likely to disappear during our lifetime. Forecasts by Paul Kagan Associates, Inc. (Carmel, CA) call for the industry to grow from $20 billion to $30 billion in about five years, with an annually compounded revenue growth rate between 1996 and 2001 of 8.6 percent.

Foreign Exhibition

The foreign theatrical market continues to provide a significant source of revenue for theatrical distribution. Major studios have their own distribution offices in many countries, and they also cooperate with local distributors. One company, UIP, is a cooperative distribution arm of several studios; it handles the foreign releases of films made by U.S. companies. The distribution fee can vary from 25 to 45 percent.

The foreign segment continues to grow. In many cases, a film may see only moderate success in the United States but do better abroad. Some films are produced with the intention of distributing them only in foreign markets, skipping the U.S. theaters entirely. It is important to remember, though, that a moderate U.S. release still drives more foreign box office than no release at all.

Nontheatrical Exhibition

Feature films also receive considerable revenue from nontheatrical sources. Beyond domestic and foreign film rentals, these include the cable networks, home video, pay-per-view, and network television. The new technologies may be another source of revenue in the future.

As the film industry has gone through evolutionary changes, so has the nontheatrical segment. In the eighties, home video was the top growth area both in the United States and abroad. Many video companies gave filmmakers advance payments in return for the home video rights to their films. The makers of *sex, lies, and videotape* are among those who received video advances and used that money to finance the production cost of their films. The films were released to video within three to six months after their theatrical release.

The advent of strong cable networks in the late eighties and early nineties has turned the emphasis from video to cable. Many video companies have gone out of business, and advances are not as common as they once were. Cable pay-per-view channels receive films at about the same time as the video stores—generally within seven to nine months of theatrical release, although films with lackluster box office often appear sooner. Some cable channels are financing their own feature-length films. However, these films appear on television first and then usually go into foreign distribution.

The television market has turned around. Until the early 1990s, the networks bought the rights to show films before they were released to cable or video and were the first window for film release.

Now, movies appear on network television after they have gone to the other ancillary outlets and often a year or two after they appear on cable. Films often are seen on airplanes at about the same time that they appear on the networks.

Some of the other ancillary revenue sources are less certain. Even with big-budget movies, the rights to the novelization of the screenplay or to the creation of comic book versions yield only small amounts of revenue. The soundtrack of a motion picture may be separately licensed to recording companies to generate revenue. Although occasionally smaller films do generate lucrative soundtracks, the revenue is too uncertain to project ahead of time.

Technology

Producers are now exploring the sales of rights to other technologies. Although CD-ROM appeared at one time to be a significant market, that technology is now fading. Factors forecasted by the Kagan Group that will influence film demand into the next millennium are:

- Sales of digital video discs (DVDs) are projected to hit $3.4 billion by 2001 and possibly $6.8 billion worldwide.
- Direct broadcast satellite (DBS), already a force in Europe, is becoming a major delivery platform in the Asia/Pacific and Latin American markets, driving pay television and pay-perview revenues.
- The United States has made controlling piracy of intellectual property (primarily videocassettes and music CDs sold in China) a top trade policy.

THE MARKET

An independent film goes through the same process from development and preproduction through production and post-production as a studio film. In this case, however, development and preproduction may involve only one or two people. And the entrepreneur, whether producer or director, maintains control over the final product.

An independent company is one that finds its production financing outside of the studios. It may be distributed by a studio, but negative cost has been found from other sources. Many of the large production companies started with the success of a single film. Carolco was built on the success of the *Rocky* and *Rambo* films; New Line achieved prominence and clout with the *Nightmare on Elm Street* series.

The smaller production company usually raises money for one film at a time, although there may be other films in different phases of development. Many companies are owned or controlled by the creative person, such as a writer/director or writer/producer, in combination with a financial partner or group. These independents make low-budget pictures, usually in the $50,000 to $5 million range.

In the past few years, there has been a resurgence of independent filmmaking. Production companies are gearing up again, and independent distributors are returning to the market. As small companies go out of business, new ones form to take their place. Since the beginning of the nineties, independent film has been going through one of its "up" cycles. Traditionally, the fortunes of independent filmmakers have always cycled up and down from year to year. The recent success of independent films, such as *The English Patient* and *Shine*, has sent the independent segment into another growth spurt.

The specialty film market has also been growing. All across the United States are individual, independently owned theaters that maintain their own mailing lists of faithful moviegoers. Often, a film made for $500,000 or less can earn back its costs from these regulars alone. Until recently, the independently owned theaters were thought of as the home of the offbeat and unique film.

Crazed Consultant Films International feels that its first film will create a new type of moviegoer for these theaters and a new type of commercial film for the mainstream theaters. Just as Billy Bob Thornton's *Sling Blade*, found a home in both art houses and malls, so will *Thursday's Cat*. Although we expect our film to have a universal enough appeal to play the mainstream houses, at its projected budget it may begin in the specialty theaters. Because of the low budget, exhibitors may wait for the film to prove itself before providing access to screens in the larger movie houses. In addition, the smaller houses will give us a chance to expand the film on a slow basis and build awareness with the public. As word of mouth increases, both the distributor and the owners of the big theater chains will want to have the *Leonard* films in the mall theaters.

Although the company will be making films about a cat, the themes are intended to be typical genres that will appeal to a mass audience. The stories will cover romance, mystery, coming of age, and other generally popular subjects. We feel that the time has finally come for the cat genre film. Cats have been with us for 12 million years, but they have been underappreciated and underexploited, especially by Hollywood. Historically, cats have had their ups and downs. Early societies revered the cat, but later on, cats, especially black ones, were categorized with witches and burned at the stake. The motion picture industry has exploited only this latter view, often casting cats as killers or as attached in some way to the supernatural.

Recent studies have shown that the cat has become the pet of choice. The tremendous success of canine films has only increased the window of opportunity for our films. Stephen King's *Sleepwalkers*, in which cats save the heroine by attacking the supernatural beings, is a beginning. However, we plan to present cats in their true light as regular, everyday heroes with all the lightness and gaiety of other current animal cinema favorites, including dogs, pigs, and bears.

In following the tradition of the dog film genre, we are also looking down the road to cable outlets. We believe that cat programs will be the next trend in this medium. There is even talk of a cat channel.

CCFI plans to begin with a $500,000 film that would benefit from exposure through the film festival circuit. The exposure of our films at festivals and limited runs in specialty theaters in target areas will create an awareness for them with the general public. In addition, we plan to tie in sales of the *Leonard* books with the films.

Although a major studio would be a natural place to go with these films, we want to remain independent. The niche market is strong enough to support the company as an independent producer. Many dog films, such as *Beethoven*, *Bingo*, and *K-9*, have been made by major studios with significant budgets. We can make a good film at a lower budget that will attract the same audiences.

Competitive Advantages

Crazed Consultant Films International has several market advantages:

1. The two principals have experience in both the creative and business areas of motion pictures. Ms. Lotta Mogul has significant production company experience. Mr. Gimme Bucks is well versed in the independent financial arena.
2. The company is run by people who are devoted to the idea of presenting the *Leonard* stories in a cost-effective but entertaining

fashion. Their devotion to quality will create low-budget films with much higher values on the screen than their budgets would dictate.

3. CCFI controls the rights to specific books, the first of which has sold well in publication. The commercial tie-in of a book with its ready-made market of readers is important to distributors. It gives them the all-important "hook" for publicizing the film.

4. Management commits to promote the films wherever and whenever possible. Promotional appearances, tours, and interviews involving a picture's actors, director, and writers are often critical for gaining the attention and acceptance for an independent film in today's competitive marketplace.

DISTRIBUTION

Most of the marketing strategies commonly employed by independent distributors will be used to market CCFI's films. The actual marketing of the film itself is the distributor's job. It involves the representation of the film in terms of genre, the placement of advertisements in various media, the selection of a sales approach for exhibitors and foreign buyers, and the "hype" (word of mouth, promotional events, alliances with special interest groups, and so on). All of these factors are critical to a film's success.

Each major studio has its own distribution division. All marketing and other distribution decisions are made in-house. This division sends out promotional and advertising materials, arranges screenings of films, and makes deals with domestic and foreign distributors. The studios each release 15 to 25 films a year, and they occasionally acquire independent films to release. For our films, however, we will seek distribution by an independent company.

We feel that independent distributors often have the knowledge and patience to give special care to eclectic or mixed-genre films. Many independents will allow a film to find its audience slowly and methodically. However, this does not mean that independent distributors will not want to release films with mass appeal. For such films with smaller budgets and lesser names, they often have an expertise that the studios lack. In addition, by focusing their marketing and promotional efforts on a handful of primary markets, these companies are able to keep their costs relatively low. Because their focus is on fewer films, we feel that our films will receive better care than at a studio.

The first step in distributing a film is having copies made of it for motion picture presentation. The prints sent to the theaters are duplications of the "master" print, which is made from the original edited negative. A print usually costs $1,200 to $1,500, depending on the length of the film and current film stock costs. Major studio films typically are opened wide—that is, on a thousand or more screens simultaneously. The cost of prints for that type of release is more than $1 million, which is impossible for low-budget films. Although the independent distributor begins with fewer prints, several hundred may be made throughout the film's release period. While a film is in release, therefore, the total print cost can be appreciable.

The domestic territory is defined as both the United States and Canada combined. Many of the independent distributors consider the United States and Canada to be one package and prefer not to have them separated beforehand. Domestic rights refer not only to theatrical distribution but to all other media, such as video, cable, pay-per-view, and television. When a producer secures an advance from one of these media for production financing, he or she makes the deal a little less attractive to potential distributors by fractionalizing the rights. Any source of future revenue that is taken out of the potential money pie makes it more difficult for the producer to close the distribution deal.

In terms of foreign sales, there are U.S. based distributors who specialize in the rest of the world. These companies deal with networks of subdistributors in various countries. It is important to distinguish between a distributor and a foreign sales agent. If a distribution company is granted the rights to the film for the foreign markets, that company is the distributor. Generally, if the ownership of the foreign rights is retained by the producer, who grants someone only a percentage of the receipts in exchange for obtaining distribution contracts in each territory or for various media throughout the world, that person is actually a sales agent.

There is no typical distribution deal. The distribution company will take as much as it can get. It is CCFI's job to give away as little as possible. Based on industry averages, we have used a distributor fee of 34 percent of the total revenue in our projections. These percentages apply only to the revenues generated by the distributor's deals; if that company is only making foreign sales, then it takes a percentage of only foreign revenues. How much the distribution company wants depends on its participation in the entire film package. The greater the up-front expense that the company must assume, the greater the percentage of incoming revenues it will seek.

In acquiring a project, the distributor looks at the following elements, among others:

- Uniqueness of story line
- Genre
- Ability of the cast members to attract audiences or buyers on their names alone
- Past successes of the producers and/or director
- Name tie-in from another medium; for example, a best-selling novel
- Special audience segment for the type, or genre, of film
- Attached money

Our films will meet these criteria easily. Necessary to selling a film is a mix of elements, although the story is always the first concern. The exhibitors to whom the distributor sells must see something in the film that they can promote to their audiences. This changes from country to country and depends on the perspective of the buyer.

Release Strategies

The ways in which a film is distributed domestically (in the United States and Canada) vary with the size of the distribution company and the type of film. Audience segmentation is determined by critical appraisal and the likely interest that the film will generate. For example, the distributor might release a film carefully, market by market, and use revenues from the first group of theaters to finance the prints and advertising for the second group, and so on.

Independent distributors use several standard patterns of release strategies. The usual method is to release a film to a few theaters at a time and slowly take it to more theaters. A popular film may well end up in large multiplexes—but usually after the film has been out for a while. This method has two advantages. It allows unique films to receive special handling, and it allows a popular-genre, small-budget film to move as fast as its advertising budget permits.

Saturation, platform, rollout, and sequencing are variations on this theme. The film opens in a few selected theaters and moves to others throughout the country in some sort of pattern. A particular film might work best in one market because of the makeup of the population, because the film was shot there, or because residents will go to see almost anything. With good reviews, a film will continue to move through the country in one of several fashions. It might move to contiguous states, open in successive theaters based on a certain time pattern, or cascade into the markets that are expected to produce the highest revenue. Whatever method is used, the film continues to open in more and more theaters. Eventually, the number of theaters will decline, but the film will remain in distribution as long as it continues to attract audiences.

The plan for CCFI's first film is to realize sizable opening audiences (relative to the budget and theme of the film) and good reviews, then use the money and reviews to continue releasing the film in additional theaters. Clearly, no one expects a $500,000 film to sell $17 or $20 million in tickets during its first weekend—or at all. The distributor will fund the copying of more prints out of the revenues from the first couple of theaters. Advertising will work in the same way. Ads in a major city newspaper can cost anywhere between $1,000 and $10,000. As a moderate-budget film earns money, it finances the advertising in the cities in which it will open later.

A very small company may use another method of distribution: 90/10 deals are actually a booking procedure that goes hand in hand with the release of small films. The distributor makes a deal with the theater to put up 90 percent of the advertising money and take 90 percent of the gross, after the exhibitor takes an agreed-upon minimum guarantee to earn the house "nut." This type of deal could be done at other percentages, but 90/10 is common. The type of distributor that we hope to attract will probably use this procedure for our first film. As we move to the $2.5 million budget level, and certainly at the $10 million level, we will be able to move out of the specialty arena and into more chain theaters.

FINANCING

The financial projections for Crazed Consultant Films International assume a conservative level of success for each film project. Many factors affect the success of any film project, including the following:

- Innate commercial appeal
- Casting
- Direction
- Timing of release
- Distribution patterns

A film's commercial appeal is undoubtedly the single most significant factor in determining its financial success. This is closely followed in importance by the agreement that the production company has with its film distributors. However, all of these factors affect the eventual bottom line.

For the purposes of this business plan, we have used current industry results for independent films of comparable size and theme. Since there have not been significant cat films, we have used the canine films as a guide. In addition, we looked at typical independent films in the budget ranges of our proposed projects.

Any film that is a "breakout"—that is, a critical and box office hit—will be over and above the financials we show. We have not factored the blockbuster low-budget films into our numbers, as they would skew our results to the high side, causing unrealistic expectations. Should one of our films earn above-average dollars, it will increase the projected revenues, putting us ahead of our anticipated profit levels. Although the print and advertising expenditures may increase at the same time, their amount is expected to be minimal compared to the additional revenues.

To help protect CCFI and the company's investors from losses, CCFI will endeavor to secure presale, distribution, and other financing agreements. Given that this company is new, an agreement will be entered into only if it is perceived to benefit all equity investors. In a presale agreement, a foreign organization or person buys the ancillary rights (domestic or foreign) in advance. The filmmaker takes this commitment, which includes a guarantee to pay a specific amount upon delivery of the completed film, to one of several specialized entertainment banks and, if the bank accepts the commitment, is able to raise money to finance production. In exchange for the presale contract, the U.S. or foreign buyer obtains the right to keep the revenue (rentals) from a particular territory and may also seek equity participation. The agreement can be for a certain length of time, a revenue cap, or both.

THE FINANCING PLAN

This section contains CCFI's sales projections and income statements for the five years beginning with production financing. The projections are based on the history of other films as well as current trends in the industry. The following are significant elements of our forecast:

1. The Company seeks capitalization equal to the full budget of $20 million. All development and production data start from the date of capitalization with funds in the bank.
2. Box Office reflects gross dollars of ticket sales before the exhibitor splits the total with the distributor. Domestic Rentals reflect the distributor's share of the box office split with the exhibitor. Domestic Ancillary includes home video, cable, network television, and television syndication. Foreign Revenue includes all monies returned to distributors from all venues outside the U.S. and Canada.
3. All funds flow from each revenue source to the distributor, who deducts his prints and ads expense and, generally, pays back the production cost before any money goes to the producer/investor line. The gross profit, therefore, is shown as the Distributor Gross Profit. The distributor's fees are not shown in the first three tables, as we have no way of knowing the details of those contracts.
4. A one-year period from start of principal photography to distribution release is projected for each film. Although new technologies may make the actual time shorter, there is no precedent for changing this standard production period.
5. The Budget, also known as the film's "negative costs," covers only the expenses that are needed to create the master print of each film. All marketing costs are included under P&A (Prints and Advertising), often referred to as "releasing costs" or "distribution expenses." These expenses also include the costs of making copies of the print from the master, advertising, video duplication, and other marketing costs.
6. The films shown in Tables 1, 2, and 3 have been used as the basis for projections in Table 5. The rationale for the projections is explained below.
7. The three profit scenarios shown in Table 5 are based on a moderate result. Whereas revenues are projected on a conservative basis, production costs are considered to be on the high side to avoid any possibility of financial shortfall.
8. Distribution Fees (the distributor's share of the revenues as compared to his expenses, which represent out-of-pocket costs) are based on 34 percent of all distributor gross revenue, both domestic and foreign, a generally accepted estimate by industry analysts and trade papers. (Note: The exhibitor's portion has been removed before this calculation.) Distribution

deals are based on negotiation and vary greatly. There is no "typical" deal. This estimate takes into account that film-makers with moderate experience have little leverage with distributors; nevertheless, the Company will seek to negotiate the most advantageous deal possible.

9. Advances from presales to foreign territories, video, cable, and free and syndicated television will be accepted when it is in CCFI's best interest.

10. Because of the timing of the cash requirements needed to produce and distribute CCFI's films, substantial amounts of the initial capital will be deposited in an interest-bearing account to be drawn as needed.

11. Net Producer/Investor Income represents the projected profit after the distributor's expenses and fees have been deducted.

12. The cash flow assumptions (Table 6) are:

(a) Film production will take a year from preproduction through post-production, ending with the creation of a master print. The actual release date depends on finalization of distribution arrangements, which may occur either before or after the film has been completed and is an unknown variable at this time. For purposes of the cash flow, we have assumed distribution will start within the first quarter after completion of the film.

(b) The majority of revenues will come back to the producers within two years after release of the film, although a smaller amount of ancillary revenues will take longer to occur and will be covered by the investor's agreement. The producers will seek an advance from the distributor as part of any deal to at least cover the investment, allowing for an earlier recoupment (and perhaps profit) than the tables show. However, it is considered an advance, and, as such, will be deducted from later profits before additional profits are paid to the producers. Because of this, Tables 5 and 6 do not reflect payment of any advance.

(c) The cumulative totals should be considered book entries, as the distributor will usually issue statements and payments every six months or once a year.

13. Completion bonds, which provide an insurance policy for the film, are not always available for low-budget films. We will make every attempt to secure one.

14. **RISK FACTORS:** The business of producing and exploiting low-cost theatrical release films is highly speculative, with many risks uncommon to other businesses. No assurances can be given of the economic success of any motion picture. The revenues derived from the production and distribution of a motion picture depend primarily upon its acceptance by the public, which cannot be predicted. In addition, the competitive nature of the film industry, the possible box office failure of a motion picture being distributed, and the potential inability of a distributor to distribute the motion picture properly, collect distribution revenues, or remit funds properly to CCFI make the successful distribution of any motion picture subject to substantial risk. The commercial success of a motion picture also depends on general economic factors and other tangible and intangible factors, all of which can change our forecasts and cannot be predicted with certainty.

The entertainment industry in general, and the motion picture industry in particular, are continuing to undergo significant changes, primarily due to technological developments. Although these developments have resulted in the availability of alternative and competing forms of leisure time entertainment, such technological developments have also resulted in the creation of additional revenue sources through licensing of rights to such new media, and potentially could lead to future reductions in the costs of producing and distributing motion pictures. In addition, the theatrical success of a motion picture remains a crucial factor in generating revenues in other media such as videocassettes and television. Because of the rapid growth of technology, shifting consumer tastes, and the popularity and availability of other forms of entertainment, it is impossible to predict the overall effect these factors will have on the potential revenue from and profitability of feature-length motion pictures.

Table A.1 Selected Films with Budgets under $1 Million ($ millions)

| Films | Revenue | | | | Cost | | | Distributor Gross Profit |
| | Domestic | | Foreign | Total | Budget | P & A | Total | |
	Rentals	Ancillary						
Nonanimal 1	1.0	1.9	2.1	5.0	0.5	1.2	1.7	3.3
Nonanimal 2	5.8	13.0	11.0	29.8	0.2	3.0	3.2	26.6
Nonanimal 3	1.0	1.7	0.8	3.5	0.1	2.0	2.1	1.4
Nonanimal 4	1.1	2.0	3.0	6.1	0.3	1.5	1.8	4.3
Nonanimal 5	2.5	3.0	1.2	6.7	0.1	2.5	2.6	4.1
Nonanimal 6	3.2	3.4	5.0	11.6	0.7	4.0	4.7	6.9
Nonanimal 7	0.4	0.9	0.8	2.1	0.1	1.5	1.6	0.5
Nonanimal 8	0.2	0.8	2.0	3.0	0.6	1.5	2.1	0.9
Nonanimal 9	1.4	2.1	0.6	4.1	0.4	1.9	2.3	1.8

Table A.2 Animal Films with Budgets of $1 to $5 Million ($ millions)

Films	Revenue				Cost			Distributor Gross Profit
	Domestic		Foreign	Total	Budget	P & A	Total	
	Rentals	Ancillary						
Bowwow 1	7.2	10.0	17.3	34.5	5.0	12.5	17.5	17.0
Bowwow 2	0.8	5.0	2.5	8.3	1.2	2.5	3.7	4.6
My Life as a Ferret	2.9	2.0	7.5	12.4	1.0	5.0	6.0	6.4
Doggie 1	1.2	9.0	12.0	22.2	1.0	0.2	1.2	21.0
Doggie 2	4.3	3.0	2.0	9.3	3.0	2.0	5.0	4.3
Rats Inc.	8.0	6.0	5.0	19.0	2.3	4.5	6.8	12.2
Pigs Galore	4.6	7.5	8.0	20.1	3.0	1.0	4.0	16.1
Fred in Heat	1.0	3.3	2.0	6.3	4.0	1.8	5.8	0.5
Sam Eats Shoes	2.4	3.5	6.6	12.5	4.5	5.0	9.5	3.0
50 Schnauzers	4.8	6.5	5.0	16.3	5.0	11.0	16.0	0.3

Table A.3 Animal Films with Budgets of $5 to $15 Million ($ millions)

| Films | Revenue | | | | Cost | | | Distributor Gross Profit |
| | Domestic | | Foreign | Total | Budget | P & A | Total | |
	Rentals	Ancillary						
Dog Came for Dinner	10.0	15.0	20.0	45.0	9.0	8.0	17.0	28.0
Jeff & His Dobie	21.0	50.0	75.0	146.0	10.0	15.0	25.0	121.0
Cathy's Cow	6.0	8.0	16.0	30.0	8.4	7.0	15.4	14.6
The Pig Pen	2.5	5.0	8.5	16.0	6.7	3.0	9.7	6.3
Cat-A-Tonic	5.7	6.8	12.0	24.5	7.0	6.5	13.5	11.0
Fido & Fluffy	6.0	12.0	17.0	35.0	5.5	6.0	11.5	23.5
Billy Beaver	18.0	10.0	45.0	73.0	6.5	15.0	21.5	51.5
Pekingese Love	14.0	7.0	12.5	33.5	9.4	11.6	21.0	12.5
Walter of Wisconsin	8.0	17.0	33.0	58.0	8.0	10.0	18.0	40.0

Table A.4 Crazed Consultant Films, Administrative Expenses
($ thousands)

Expenses	Start-up	Year One	Year Two	Year Three	Year Four	Year Five
Salaries						
Executive Producer*	40.0	50.0	50.0	50.0	50.0	50.0
V.P. Financial*	30.0	40.0	40.0	40.0	40.0	40.0
Development	12.0	25.0	35.0	35.0	35.0	35.0
Secretary	6.0	18.0	22.0	25.0	30.0	33.0
General						
Office Expenses	1.2	2.5	2.5	2.5	2.5	2.5
Telephones/Fax	1.5	3.0	3.5	3.5	3.5	3.5
Professional Fees	6.0	10.0	10.0	10.0	10.0	10.0
Travel/Entertainment	7.0	5.0	5.0	6.0	6.0	7.0
Option	5.0					
Additional Payments —Author		50.0		50.0	50.0	
Computer	3.0		1.0		1.0	
Furniture/Equipment	2.5					
Printing	3.0	2.0	2.0	2.0	2.0	2.0
Seminars	4.0	5.0	5.0	5.0	5.0	5.0
Total Administrative Expense	**121.2**	**210.5**	**176.0**	**229.0**	**235.0**	**188.0**

*Equity participants.

Table A.5 Estimated Income Statement for Three Films over Five Years ($ thousands)

Films	Revenue				Initial Costs			Distributor Gross Profit	Estimated Distributor Fees	Producer Gross Income	Company Overhead	Net Producer/ Investor Income
	Domestic		Foreign	Total	Budget	P & A	Total					
	Rentals	Ancillary										
Thursday's Cat	960	3,100	3,000	7,060	500	1,350	1,850	5,210	2,400	2,810	31	2,779
Nine Lives of Leonard	3,600	6,380	8,300	18,280	2,500	4,000	6,500	11,780	6,215	5,565	179	5,386
Leonard in Space	14,400	19,500	43,125	77,025	10,000	20,000	30,000	47,025	26,189	20,836	76	20,760

Table A.6 Crazed Consultant Films, Projected Cash Flow by Quarter, Years One to Five ($ millions)

	Year 1				Year 2				Year 3				Year 4				Year 5			
	Qtr. 1	Qtr. 2	Qtr. 3	Qtr. 4	Qtr. 1	Qtr. 2	Qtr. 3	Qtr. 4	Qtr. 1	Qtr. 2	Qtr. 3	Qtr. 4	Qtr. 1	Qtr. 2	Qtr. 3	Qtr. 4	Qtr. 1	Qtr. 2	Qtr. 3	Qtr. 4
Thursday's Cat																				
Production	(0.1)	(0.2)	(0.1)	(0.1)																
Prints and Ads					(0.7)	(0.3)	(0.2)	(0.1)												
Domestic Rentals					0.3	0.4	0.2	0.1												
Domestic Ancillary						1.0	0.5			1.0	0.5									
Foreign Revenue							0.9	0.7	0.5	0.7	0.2									
Distributor Fees					(0.2)	(0.6)	(0.6)	(0.1)	(0.2)	(0.2)	(0.4)	(0.1)								
Nine Lives of Leonard																				
Production					(0.6)	(0.8)	(0.3)													
Prints and Ads									(2.1)	(1.0)	(0.5)	(0.4)								
Domestic Rentals									1.1	1.3	0.8	0.4								
Domestic Ancillary										2.1	1.1		2.1	1.1						
Foreign Revenue											2.4	2.0	1.2	2.0	0.7					
Distributor Fees									(0.6)	(1.5)	(1.4)	(0.2)	(0.6)	(0.5)	(0.9)	(0.5)				
Leonard in Space																				
Production							(2.5)	(3.0)	(3.0)	(1.5)										
Prints and Ads											(10.6)	(5.0)	(2.6)	(1.8)						
Domestic Rentals												4.3	5.3	3.4	1.4					
Domestic Ancillary													6.4	3.3			6.4	3.4		
Foreign Revenue														12.6	10.3	6.5	10.3	3.4		
Distributor Fees												(2.5)	(6.3)	(6.0)	(0.8)	(2.6)	(2.1)	(5.8)		
Totals	**(0.1)**	**(0.2)**	**(0.1)**	**(0.1)**	**(1.2)**	**(0.3)**	**(2.5)**	**(2.7)**	**(4.3)**	**0.9**	**(7.9)**	**(1.5)**	**3.4**	**15.1**	**11.8**	**3.4**	**14.6**	**1.0**		
Cumulative Total	**(0.1)**	**(0.3)**	**(0.4)**	**(0.5)**	**(1.7)**	**(2.0)**	**(4.5)**	**(7.2)**	**(11.5)**	**(10.6)**	**(18.5)**	**(20.0)**	**(16.6)**	**(1.5)**	**10.3**	**13.7**	**28.3**	**29.3**		

Totals may not add due to rounding.

Index

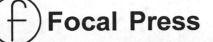 **Focal Press**

Focal Press

(f) Focal Press

Related Titles

Digital Filmmaking
The Changing Art and Craft of
Making Motion Pictures
by *Thomas A. Ohanian and Michael E. Phillips*

This comprehensive book on the subject of digital filmmaking features interviews with leading filmmakers including James Cameron and George Lucas. It is the professional "bible" of the new era in filmmaking and details the procedural, creative, and technical aspects of preproduction, production, and post-production within a digital filmmaking environment.

1996 • pa • 298pp • 0-240-80219-5

Sound for Film and Television
by *Tomlinson Holman*

Provides an overall introduction to the field of recording, editing, and mixing audio for films and television programs. A balance is struck between aesthetic and technical content, combining theory and practice, to approach sound as both an art and a science, as no other text has before. Accompanying audio CD contains examples demonstrating key concepts.

April 1997 • pa • 252pp w/audio CD • 0-240-80291-8

Media Law for Producers
Third Edition
by *Phillip Miller*

Cuts through the legalese and illustrates legal issues to help producers recognize the legal questions that can come up during production – from performer contracts through copyright registrations. Examines the court system and how media law is made.

April 1998 • pa • 288pp • 0-240-80303-5